# Rothley and the Abolition of the Slave Trade

## The mutual endeavours of Babington, Gisborne, Wilberforce and Macaulay

**Terry Sheppard**
**& Iain Whyte**

To Pam, enjoy
Terry Sheppard

Rothley History Society

Rothley History Society
17a Anthony Street
Rothley, Leicester

Set in Garamond by the Society using Serif Page Plus, and printed and bound in Great Britain by
AnchorPrint, Syston, Leicester

ISBN 0-9545426-6-5

# *Contents*

*To the people who live in Rothley,*
*and especially those on the two Roads named Babington and Macaulay, that they might take pride in two holders of these names for their unstinting efforts to abolish Britain's Slave Trade, those two hundred years ago.*


# *Acknowledgements*

Professor James Walvin, for graciously contributing his Foreword to this enterprise. The team under Jonathan Smith, who in the classical surroundings of the Wren Library at Trinity College Cambridge, were uncommonly patient and helpful with the supply of those boxes of Babington letters.

Iain Whyte, who in the middle of a hectic schedule of his own, has given much time, energy and counsel to the project, as well as the three chapters on Macaulay.

The planning group at Rothley; Peter and Sue Joyce, Brenda Sutherland, Stephen Baum, and Brian Verity, who had faith that a book could be produced in so short a space of time, and who built a commemorative event around its launch on the bicentenary day, and together with Rothley Church and others, underwrote its production. Mary Macrae, for her perceptive proof-reading. Doug Sutherland and Christopher Baines, for help with images. David Lynch, Rothley's Postmaster, who so willingly helped with the sale of this book. Olde English Inns, proprietors of the Rothley Court Hotel, for making the Hotel available for the commemoration. Charnwood Borough Council, for joining with the project to mark the bicentenary with a new plaque.

The Rothley History Society, who welcomed the book into its growing list of publications.

My wife Pauline, who saw my enforced time at the keyboard as a stage that men approaching seventy have to go through, and bore it with equanimity and encouragement.

# *Figures*

# *Foreword*

The abolition of the slave trade in 1807 marked a remarkable change of direction for the British. Once the major slave trader in the Atlantic, in 1807 the British turned their back on slave trading and henceforth became the world's leading abolitionist power. The Act of 1807 also represented a remarkable upsurge in popular sentiment: Parliament and people were as one in their decision to reject the slave trade.

It is fitting that Rothley marks that event with this publication. Like abolitionists across the country, Rothley was home both to a local campaign against the trade and a stopping point for abolitionists travelling the country and seeking to persuade Parliament to listen to the popular will. Rothley was also home to a dynasty of abolitionists, the Babingtons, who left their mark on the campaign against the trade and, later, in the renewed attack on slavery itself, abolished in 1833-38.

The story of abolition is normally told through the eyes of Parliament itself. But Parliament was forced to act in 1807 because of a series of overlapping local campaigns, like the one in Rothley, which persuaded politicians and Ministers that the slave trade had become a deeply unpopular issue. What follows is, then, a microcosm of that national campaign and an illustration of why abolition became inevitable by 1807. There were hundreds of stories, like the one in Rothley, which formed the backbone of the British campaign against the slave trade.

James Walvin
*Professor Emeritus, University of York*
*and leading historian on slavery and abolition.*

# *The Scheme*

Four separate elements came together to bring this project to fruition. As long ago as 1994, as assignments one and two in the University of Nottingham's Local History three year course, I had to pick over the landscape and sources of my local parish of Rothley, Leicestershire. It had the Knights Templars, the Knights Hospitallers, and the 300 year stewardship of the Babington family stamped all over it. The Templar's 13th century Chapel and Preceptory still stand, incorporated into the Babington manor house that is now the Rothley Court Hotel. I have long been intrigued by the last Babington to use Rothley Temple as a family home, the name they gave it. Thomas Babington died in 1837, exactly one hundred years and a day before I was born. He lived in the age of the quill pen, the horse and the carriage. He was Leicester's MP from 1800 to 1818. He did not write a political or biographical book, and no one has written a book about him. There is only one portrait still extant, guarded by the British Museum. He was a quiet, more reserved type of person, who discovered a Christian faith that took the social implications of the Gospel at face value, and brought them to bear on what he saw around him. Apart from the running and improvement of his manorial estate, Babington took up the voluntary career option of being by the side of William Wilberforce from 1788 right through until 1818 and beyond, when he left Parliament. With his brother-in-law Thomas Gisborne, of Yoxall Lodge in Staffordshire, both having met Wilberforce at Cambridge, they became Wilberforce's aides in London, and in some important summers, at Yoxall and at Rothley Temple.

The second element concerns my co-author, Iain Whyte. One Sunday in Rothley Church many moons ago, after the morning service, I discovered a distinguished couple standing in the chancel peering up at the various monuments to the Macaulay family. Iain was embarked on his own trail of discovery, gathering material for a major work on the abolition of black slavery in Scotland, and for a new study of the abolitionist Zachary Macaulay. After Iain and his wife Isabel's study semester at the Huntingdon Library in California the next year, they came back to Rothley and retold the amazing life story of

Zachary in new graphic detail, having read all the original letters collected by the Huntingdon.

Then thirdly, on a November week in 2006 when my wife went away on a course, I realised a long-held ambition to get immersed in the 51 boxes of Babington Manuscripts carefully preserved in the Wren Library at Trinity College, Cambridge. Box 13 in particular has a wealth of letters written from London by Thomas Babington to his wife Jean [nee Macaulay] at Rothley or at Yoxall. They show in graphic detail Babington and Gisborne's role in Wilberforce's London home at the height of the campaign in Parliament to abolish the Slave Trade in the 1790s.

Finally, the date of 25 March 2007 appeared on the diary horizon, 200 years since King George III signed into law the Bill to Abolish the Slave Trade in the British Empire. So in December 2006 people in Rothley Church and in the village's History Society decided that of all places, Rothley ought to mark this day. Here was an opportunity to get at least one book into print that said something about the career of this special man, Thomas Babington, against the backdrop of this extraordinary campaign to right the awful wrong of the Slave Trade. And since Thomas married a Macaulay, and was later to play a signal role in the life of his brother-in-law Zachary, to feature Zachary too. So I am greatly indebted to Iain Whyte for writing the three chapters on Macaulay, Nos. 3, 7, and 10; for fitting into the idea of this venture; and for giving such a measured and wise steer to my enthusiasm and haste.

When the commemoration at the Rothley Court Hotel is completed on 25th March 2007, and the new plaque marking the bicentenary is installed outside, there remain all those other boxes at Trinity College. Perhaps there will be a major book about the Babington family yet.

Terry Sheppard
Rothley 25 March 2007

# 1

# *A Privileged Life?*

Thomas Babington settled into his new surroundings at St John's College, Cambridge in June 1775. It was a decided step-up from his accommodation as a boarder at Rugby school, which he had joined in 1770, five years earlier. Cambridge in June was a magical place, and the ethos and life of the College admirably suited his sense of who he was. Quiet, serious minded, purposeful, with a family tradition to uphold. This was the next step in his life, destined as he was to inherit the manor and soke of Rothley as the eldest son of Thomas Babington and Lydia, daughter of Joseph Cardale, Vicar of Hinckley. This came sooner than was ideal, for in 1776 his father died, and Thomas became lord of the manor in his own right, at just 18 years old. His mother Lydia continued to look after the domestic arrangements at Rothley Temple, the family mansion, while the business of seeing to tenant affairs and collecting rents was discharged by his land agent. The Leicester solicitor John Heyrick fulfilled the role of Steward of Babington's manorial court, just like his father Samuel had done before him.

In the year his father died, Babington was joined at St John's by two young men from strong family backgrounds. He took quickly to Thomas Gisborne, the eldest son of Derby landowner John Gisborne, whose early education was at the hands of the Revd John Pickering, Vicar of nearby Mackworth. Derby was not far from Babington's home in Leicestershire, lying on the same road as would be taken by a traveller going north from Leicester. Gisborne was born the same year as Babington, 1758, and finished his schooling at Harrow between 1772 and 1776. He too would come into his inheritance before he graduated, his father John dying in 1779.[1]

The other young man occupied a study next to Gisborne, and had come to Cambridge via a mixture of schools starting with the Grammar School at Hull. His father died when he was nine, and he was sent to live with an uncle and aunt in Wimbledon, who put him in a boarding school in Putney. In the vacations this young man had opportunity to listen to sermons of the evangelical sort, especially at the feet of the personable ex-sea captain and slave trader Revd John Newton, who added 279 hymns to the music canon including Amazing Grace.[2] With his mother becoming alarmed by the content of the letters from her son William, Mrs Robert Wilberforce determined that she would come south by coach to rescue William from the possibility of his 'turning Methodist'. And as she judged that his old Master at Hull Grammar, Joseph Milner, had also 'turned Methodist', the young William was packed off to his grandfather's old boarding school at Pocklington, a village near York, with a distant view of York Minster.[3] William later wrote that being wrenched away from his uncle and aunt 'affected me most seriously. It almost broke my heart, I was so attached to them'.[4] The Wilberforces were rich Baltic Traders operating out of England's fourth largest port, Hull. When William's father Robert died, Abel Smith became head of the business, changing its name to Wilberforce and Smith. Abel Smith was a 'younger son of the banker of Nottingham whose numerous descendants have been important in banking ever since'. William Wilberforce became so well endowed from the family fortune and business that he could decide to avoid earning a living for the rest of his life.

This was the William Wilberforce who came up to St John's Cambridge and took up that study next to Gisborne in October 1776. William Pitt the younger had also come to Cambridge that year, but he was over at Pembroke, though he and Wilberforce became acquainted. Wilberforce had a different approach to using the time at Cambridge from Babington and Gisborne. He placed a high value on socialising, a habit that was not corrected by his tutor, who did not urge Wilberforce to attend lectures. In the years to come Wilberforce would rue not being taught to work hard by his tutors. 'But for a natural love of classical learning, and that it was necessary for a man to be publicly examined to avoid being disgraced, I should have done nothing all the time I was at Cambridge'.[5] Wilberforce would return to his room in the evening and summon Gisborne to join him 'by the music of his poker and tongs played out on our back-to-back chimney pieces or by the melodious challenge of his voice'.[6] Gisborne went on, 'he was so winning and amusing that I often sat up with him half the night to the detriment of my attendance at lectures the next day'. It would be the warmth of this interaction that would bring Gisborne to Wilberforce's aid in later times.

Gisborne worked harder and with direction. He had determined on a career in holy orders, winning the chancellor's medal in classics, graduating BA sixth wrangler in 1780. Although Gisborne had the intellect and connections to pursue a career in high public office, he chose instead the life of a country parson, where he had time and space to pursue a writing career.[7] This would point to Gisborne having a reflective disposition, commenting on society and politics from a position one step outside the front line of the action. Babington was of a similar ilk. When Gisborne and Babington came together later to work directly alongside the outgoing and upfront Wilberforce, it would be these qualities of quiet reflection that would be just the foil that Wilberforce needed. When considering his future, Babington had to bear in mind that he had a large, unimproved agricultural estate to manage, with the extended responsibility for supervising the several parishes making up the soke of Rothley. He must have judged, or taken advice, that to have a legal qualification would be of most value. So he read law alongside the classics and mathematics and in 1778 was admitted to Lincoln's Inn, though he never practised as a solicitor. Babington graduated BA twelfth wrangler in 1779.[8]

The Babington and Gisborne friendship prospered. By 1783 Gisborne, now in holy orders, had taken up residence in Yoxall Lodge, Staffordshire, inherited from his father, and was given the perpetual curacy of nearby Barton under Needwood by the Bishop of Lichfield in the same year. In 1784 Gisborne married Babington's sister Mary, forging an enduring link between the two Cambridge men.

Chapter Notes:

1 *Oxford Dictionary for National Biography*, (2004), entry for Thomas Gisborne.
2 Although John Newton was Vicar of Olney in Buckinghamshire, he was a regular and celebrated preacher at London venues.
3 John Pollock, *William Wilberforce,* (London 1982), p.4.
4 Samuel, S, *Fragments of his Father's Conversation*, Bodleian Library, Oxford e.11, f.122.
5 Ibid, f.126
6 Quoted in Harford, John, *Recollections of William Wilberforce*, p.201.
7 *ONDB*, Thomas Gisborne.
8 Ibid, Thomas Babington.

*Gate Panel at St John's College Cambridge*

# 2

# *Losing a Heart*

Thomas Babington now turned his attention to improving his estate, determining to modernise the open field system that lay at its core. Over the two years to 1782, his Rothley Enclosure Act reached the statute book and much of the modernisation was well in hand. Several new farm complexes were constructed, including his home farm bearing the imprint 'TB 1781', picked out in blue bricks on the side of the big barn, alongside the turnpike. Another farm that came to be known as Rothley Lodge, overlooking the Soar Valley and the meadows towards Mountsorrel, was awarded to the Vicar of Rothley in lieu of tithes. A ten acre piece in the old South Field was given to the Wardens of the parish church, in lieu of a variety of small corners previously held in the open field system. The open landscape was now marked out in orderly fields, with the new hedging already growing into its place. Babington also began to make his mark in the County. He served the customary year as the Sheriff of Leicestershire in 1780/81, and was appointed a magistrate.

With that accomplished, Babington must have thought a little about the normal thing that happens to single country gentlemen who head a significant estate. They usually make a marriage, from which comes the next generation who will carry on the family name and inherit the estate. Gisborne was regularly at Rothley Temple, with Babington's sister Mary becoming more thrilled each time he came. In the end, Babington had to tell Gisborne that his visits were too unsettling for his sister and that he had better do something about the relationship or curtail his visits. They went on to make a very happy marriage, and the bond between the families at Yoxall Lodge and Rothley Temple became very strong.

Writing in 1875 in a country house reminiscence piece, Babington's granddaughter Eliza Coneybeare tells the story of what happened next to Babington.

> 'My Grandfather, I believe, had several small love affairs, and one, when he was about twenty-five, which went very deep. Such a bungling mess as foolish friends and his own sensitiveness made of it. One ounce of common good sense in any would have prevented the heart-break, for the lady and himself. As it was, after a long shilly shally, she went and married somebody else, and my Grandfather with a sore heart set off on a riding tour to Scotland to recover his spirits. Amongst the various introductions which he took with him to Scotland was one to a Mr. Macaulay, the Scotch minister of a church near Inverary and occupier of the manse. Here he was received very cordially, and here he stayed off and on for some time. I have myself read a letter from him written thence, describing how he stayed and read Milton to the daughters while they span, and how there was one young girl of exquisite sensibility, etc. My Grandfather was always especially attracted by quick sympathy in a woman, and quick sympathy my dear Grandmother assuredly possessed'.[1]

Eliza's recollection of Babington's age is suspect at 25, as his trip to Scotland was made in 1787. Babington fell for this daughter of the manse, Jean Macaulay, and they were married on 8 October 1787.[2]

So Babington lost his heart twice. The rather shy, reflective person seemingly was not able to be decisive enough to win his first real love. Eliza Coneybeare's code of 'quick sympathy' probably means that Jean was more outgoing and direct, taking the initiative, allowing Thomas to feel warmed and able to respond. The 'introductions' that Babington took with him to Scotland to call at the Macaulay manse at Cardross came from the Revd Aulay Macaulay, a son of that manse, then the Vicar of Claybrooke in Leicestershire. Aulay and Babington were friends, part of the circle of evangelicals in Leicestershire. It was likely to Aulay that Babington confessed his heartache over the loss of his first love. Aulay would have prescribed the medicine of a jaunt to Scotland, to clear his head and restore his spirits. Eliza Coneybeare's writings conflate what actually happened, since it is clear that Aulay actually accompanied Babington on his tour,[3] which is understandable, since Babington would need a guide, and Aulay would have relished such a visit to his country of birth and to his family.

There were strains when Babington brought his new wife home to Rothley Temple. Eliza Coneybeare continues the story:

> 'Well they were married, and he brought her home, very young and very unformed, to his stately English home. My Grandmother has often described to me her arrival, and all the servants drawn up to receive her, and her first impression of her dignified and somewhat formal mother and sister-in-law. For a time she remained very quiet, simply observing. I only remember her as the most fascinating of hostesses, her household admirably arranged, and by excellent management keeping a table at which Kings and Princes might rejoicingly sit down, and at small expense. But at her first arrival there was bitter disappointment in old Mrs. Babington's mind at the bride her son had chosen. My Grandmother has described to me her discarded feeling of sitting on one side on the evening of her arrival, my Grandfather having had to leave her to settle business with his steward. For the next two or three years, while the mother lived, they spent quite half their time at Yoxall Lodge'.

Here again Eliza's second-hand recollection misses the essential but charming truth of the story. Babington's mother indeed had her disappointment but that was at the time of hearing the news of the engagement from Scotland. Babington knew that the lovely girl he had lost his heart to had grown up in a quiet manse, and faced a steep learning curve to be able to hold down the task of running a busy English country home. After the marriage, he took his bride to Yoxall Lodge in Staffordshire where over the next six months she absorbed the necessary skills under the care of Babington's sister, Mary Gisborne. Only when her 'probationary period'[4] was over at the end of six months, and 'she was judged capable of taking the head of her own house', did the couple return to Rothley Temple. But Jean's charm and verve had won them all over, and Babington's mother settled back into the household at Rothley under her daughter-in-law with affectionate contentment.

The learning curve was not just about running a house. It was clearly felt important that a country house lady should have informed opinions about matters of the day, and should be able to write in a graceful way. This was all as well as the traditional role of childbearing. Writing from London in February 1788 to the four month's pregnant Jean during her 'probationary period' at Yoxall, Babington gives instruction on how to address a letter ('write the directions'), and was 'pleased to hear you have been blooded'.[5] Eight days later Babington writes about being in the public gallery of the Commons with Gisborne, and marvelling at Pitt's speech. They were to 'dine that night with Wilberforce'. In the letter the loving husband 'urges his wife to continue reading the Paper of the Mirror each day', and so 'continue to improve your pronunciation and manner of reading' and become 'mistress of the author's ideas'.[6] It looks as if a West Highland accent was being gently toned down to suit English ears.

Then there were the writing skills. The next day Babington was pleased to hear 'that you are better. This Magnesia, it is hoped, will prove a fortunate discovery, and be of great use to you'.[7] Adjusting to an English diet may have been difficult for Jean's digestion, probably compounded by morning sickness. The letter continues: 'You must write slowly and carefully, my dear, or I will see you will get back into a bad hand again; this would give me great concern as you know what trouble it has cost both you and me to improve it. Should you like to undergo all this labour another time?' 'You must be aware my dear how necessary it is for a woman to write *decently* and how great an ornament it is for her if she writes with a degree of *neatness* and *elegance*.' One can picture the scene at Yoxall in the Library: Babington and Jean gently working with their quill pens practicing laying out neat and graceful script in well spaced straight lines!

Wilberforce began to lose his heart in a different way. He was not attracted to a life of study and scholarship; neither did the idea of getting involved in the family business appeal, especially as it would have meant 'submitting himself to his Smith cousins'. He used the summer vacation of 1779 to enjoy being 'agreeably idle' in a series of visits to country houses, and in the autumn was in Cambridge from time to time. The winter of 1779-80 saw him often in London without much direction, save that he and William Pitt often met in the gallery of the House of Commons, listening to the debates, their acquaintance blossoming into friendship. Pitt was much more earnest, 'reading hard for the bar', as a basis for a future political career. Pitt urged Wilberforce to chum up with him in the House 'as soon as they could get seats'. This opportunity came sooner for the 'indolent amateurish' Wilberforce than it did for the 'professionally minded' Pitt.

Back at his Hull home in the spring of 1780 the talk of an imminent general election put the idea in Wilberforce's mind that he could stand for the borough of Hull. He would have to convince the electorate of 1,100, most of whom were hereditary freemen, out of a total population exceeding 15,000. Hull returned two members, and as was the prevailing climate, the customary bribe to the electors was 'two guineas a vote'. Each elector had two votes. All summer in 1780 Wilberforce 'coaxed them with his charm and his purse',[8] spending the massive sum of £8,000 on the campaign. On 12 September the result was declared, Wilberforce had amassed 1,126 votes, the same number as the other two candidates together. In his own contest Pitt had stood for Cambridge University but failed to get elected. He entered the House in the following January on a by-election for a Lowther borough and actually made his maiden speech before Wilberforce. Two 'boys' in the House, but with an eloquence and independence far beyond their years.

Wilberforce had not yet found his heart however. At the end of the short parliamentary session in 1784 he went off in the summer with his family for the season at Scarborough. There he 'fell in with the huge Isaac Milner, his old usher at Hull Grammar School, who was now a tutor at Queens College, Cambridge'. Wilberforce had resolved to winter on the Riviera for his mother's and sister's health, but had yet to find a travelling companion for himself. 'On impulse, he invited Milner, all expenses paid'. Milner was now a clergyman at Cambridge, and was able to negotiate leave of absence from his college and the party crossed the channel on October 20th, 1784, taking two carriages. All through France the two men argued and disputed moral, ethical and religious ideas. Though not exhibiting what would usually be taken as the behaviour of a 'serious Christian', Milner's brilliant mind had a good grasp of the 'intellectual heart of Christianity', but not to much avail however with the sceptical Wilberforce during the outward journey or while staying on the Riviera.

Very early in the year Wilberforce received a 'long and affectionate letter' from Pitt. Wilberforce was urged to return to the house for the day when Pitt would introduce his measure for Parliamentary Reform.[9] With the ladies nicely set up on the Riviera, Milner and Wilberforce set off in the chaise, Wilberforce 'casually picking up a book given to him by Bessie Smith'. The pair now had something external to anchor their discussions. The book, *The Rise and Progress of Religion in the Soul* by Phillip Doddridge, who had 'taught his students in Northamptonshire the great reformation doctrine of Justification by Faith before Whitfield recovered it for the multitudes in Hanoverian England'. The book and the discussions with Milner began the change of heart in Wilberforce. 'By the time Milner deposited him on 22 February 1785 at No. 10 Downing Street, Wilberforce had reached intellectual assent to the Biblical view of man, God, and Christ. He thrust it to the back of his mind and resumed his social and political life'.

In June 1785 before the house adjourned, Wilberforce and Milner resumed their chaise-borne dialogue on their way back south to join the ladies at Genoa, then moving on through Switzerland to settle for six weeks in September at Spa in Austria. At the end of hours of reading and debating the New Testament in Greek, Wilberforce now shifted his position to 'fully believing the Gospel'. Not that it stopped him from joining in the 'cosmopolitan junketings with the old abandon, except that he would not go to the theatre or travel on Sundays.' He concluded that because his heart was split between the worldly and the serious then 'in the true sense of the word I am not a Christian', and he began to sicken of the 'profligacy and selfish luxury of the rich, of the hours wasted in eating'.[10] By the third week of October 1785, Wilberforce's heart had moved into the 'crisis of the classic Christian tradition'. He had the choice to make, between 'Christ and the world. He wanted both'.

Back in England Wilberforce's crisis and anguish of spirit led him to correspond with Pitt in tones that implied a retreat from political life, to Pitt's alarm. Wilberforce turned to his boyhood hero, the Revd John Newton, now at 60 the Rector of St Mary Woolnoth in the City. A secret meeting was arranged, for Wilberforce feared earning the then 'fashionable world's contempt of evangelicals' if he was seen calling on the old parson. Newton was a calming influence, urging Wilberforce not to cut himself off from his present circles or to retire from public life. Some words written two years later to Wilberforce might have reinforced what he said on that day: 'It is hoped and believed that the Lord has raised you up for the good of his church and for the good of the nation'.[11]

Wilberforce went away to Pitt's newly acquired house Holwood in Kent lighter in spirit. The sense of being redeemed was now in ascendance over the sense of guilt. Wilberforce made one more trip in this mood, this time into Essex to meet the Revd William Unwin, the donor of the Doddridge book to Bessie Smith's mother. Pollock describes Wilberforce's Easter Day 1786 experience like this: Soon after sunrise the member for Yorkshire took to the fields to pray and give thanks 'amidst the general chorus with which all nature seems on such a morning to be swelling the song of praise and thanksgiving'.[12]

Chapter Notes:

1 Eliza Coneybeare, *Rothley Temple in the Olden Time*, box 50, Babington MSS at Trinity College, Cambridge.
2 *ONDB*, Thomas Babington.
3 Trevelyan, G.O., *The Life and Letters of Lord Macaulay*, Harper, (New York, 1876), p.23. The author was a great nephew of Zachary Macaulay and son of Zachary and Selina's seventh child, Hannah More Macaulay.

Trevelyan writes of Aulay: "Of all his undertakings the one best deserving commemoration in these pages was a tour he made into Scotland with Thomas Babington....in the course of which the travellers paid a visit to the manse at Cardross".

4 Knutsford, Viscountess, *The Life and Letters of Zachary Macaulay*, (London, 1900), p.14.

5 TB in London to Jean B at Yoxall, 14 Feb 1788, Babington MSS, 13.8.

6 Ibid, TB to JB, 23 Feb 1788, 13.14.

7 Ibid, TB to JB, 23 feb 1788, 13.15.

8 Pollock, p.11.

9 Wilberforce, A. M., ed., *Private Papers of William Wilberforce*, quoted in Pollock, p.34.

10 Fragments, f.132

***Rothley Temple.*** *The late 18th century image of Babington's Home as originally published in Nichols' History and Antiquities of the County of Leicester, Volume III. The 13th Century Preceptory and Chapel of the Knights Templar forms the right hand third of the structure.*

*The extension to the left was undertaken after the Babington family became the owners and lords of the manor in the second half of the 16th Century. The famous son of Zachary and Selina Macaulay who became Baron Macaulay of Rothley was born in the first floor end room on the left.*

# 3

# *Highland Manse to Jamaican Plantation*

On 2 May 1768 a boy was born to Rev. John and Mrs. Margaret Macaulay (nee Campbell) in the Church of Scotland manse in Inverary in Argyll. The Macaulays were from Harris, inheritors of Gaelic language and folklore, and no less than four of John's brothers were ministers of the Church. Margaret Campbell was a clanswoman of the Duke of Argyll whose family seat was in the town and who held the patronage of the parish church. We have already seen how closely linked with Rothley the Macaulay family were to become on account of Thomas Babington's friendship with Aulay and through him to Jean Macaulay, after her father had moved to take the charge of Cardross near Dumbarton; yet it was this younger brother Zachary who of all the family, despite a very rocky start, was to leave the most indelible mark on the movement for the abolition of the slave trade and slavery.

Rev. John Macaulay was a staunch Calvinist and an equally staunch opponent of the Jacobite cause and supporter of the Settlement of 1690.[1] He was a stern and remote figure and although he strongly encouraged learning in his sons, especially in the classics, he showed little affection towards his family. The family moved south when Zachary was six years old, but not before he had imbibed something of highland folklore that sat in an uneasy alliance with Calvinist theology. Later in life this curious mixture was to shape his thinking. He was a voracious reader and had a passion from early years for language and literature, devouring many volumes in his father's library. But a minister's stipend could not support the education of such a large family and instead of going to University, as he had hoped, Zachary at 14 years of age was found a position in the counting-house of a merchant house in Glasgow.

In a long journal written to his fiancée fifteen years later Zachary confessed to this period of his life as 'a career of vice and folly.'[2] Perhaps frustrated by his lack of formal University education he spent a great deal of time with students, loved debates and arguments, was seduced by the pleasures of drink and the fashionable scepticism over religion and neglected much that he had been brought up to revere. He did not neglect books however and added some of the new novels to his repertoire. But in late 1784 some unspecified situation, described as a 'labyrinth,' possibly involving a woman, led to his extrication from the Glasgow merchants and onto to a boat bound for Jamaica.[3]

Scots were active at all levels on the plantations of the West Indian slave islands. Edward Long the Jamaican historian estimated that one third of the white population of the largest Caribbean colonies in 1780 were from 'North Britain' and he added 'and such is their industry and address that few of them have been disappointed.'[4] Young Zachary was one of many who sought a new start through the colonies. Slavery and the slave trade were being questioned by the intellectuals of the Enlightenment but the urgent needs of employment or wealth creation tended to outweigh any scruples. After all, Robert Burns, who wrote 'The Slave's Lament,' was at the same time set to become a manager of slaves on a Jamaican estate, until the first major edition of his poems in 1786 provided a respite from poverty. Macaulay had no such alternative skill. But a relative, Sir Archibald Campbell, former Governor of Jamaica promised his father to set up contacts on the island. In the end these proved worthless and young Zachary at sixteen was thrown on his own resources.

Historians are generally agreed that plantation slavery in the West Indies was harder and more brutal than in Virginia or the American colonies and of all the islands Jamaica was the worst. In a pamphlet published in 1823 Zachary Macaulay detailed conditions for slaves on the islands, as he was to do with great effect throughout the later abolition campaign.[5] The average length of life for slaves who survived the horrors of the transatlantic journey was five to seven years. Few saw old age and those who did were termed 'worn out slaves' and frequently abandoned to starvation. From sunrise to sunset and often into the night, slaves on the sugar plantations were all too often worked to death, and simply replaced when the next shipment of human cargo docked. James Ramsay, a pioneer abolitionist, who gave Wilberforce his early evidence, argued that constant fear of rebellion by greatly superior numbers was the key reason for Africans in the West Indies being treated far worse than animals.[6] The floggings, tortures, and mutilations, often the result of a depraved society, were seen as necessary tools of terror in a system that gave no legal or other protection to humans who were classed as 'property,' to be bought, sold, and used at will.

Records of ruthless regimes in our time, from Nazi Europe to the killing fields of Cambodia, demonstrate how otherwise decent people collude with the horror. Macaulay's journal illustrates very clearly how survival for those of the ruling race in the Caribbean necessitated the blunting of sensibilities and the suppression of human feelings. In 1785 he had written to a friend in Scotland that he was hardly recognisable 'were you to view me in a field of canes, amidst perhaps a hundred of the sable race, cursing and bawling, while the noise of the whip resounding on their shoulders, and the cries of the poor wretches would make you imagine some unlucky accident had carried you to the doleful shades.'

This ironic and even sympathetic account of the fate of the slaves was soon, by Zachary's own admission, overshadowed by his accommodation to the ethos of the master group. He described it as 'waging war with my taste and feelings' but for him, with no other means of support, there was no middle ground between accommodating to his lot and starving. He therefore 'resolved to get rid of my squeamishness' and in a recollection that was to haunt him all his life, Macaulay spoke of his callousness towards the sufferings of the slaves which he could speak about 'with a levity which sufficiently marked my depravity.'[7]

The Jamaican testimony of this young man demonstrated a barrenness of soul. His religion was as cold as his relationships with others. In repeated illness, when he often felt terrified by the prospect of death, he sought no help from friends and received none. In health, he equally separated himself from others, feeling superior to them but behaving no better. Despite earlier misgivings he had become so accommodated to Jamaica that he hesitated before accepting the offer of an uncle in London to return to Britain in 1789. But not to Scotland; his father had died that year and his mother was to survive for only a few more months. Instead this twenty-one year old young man from the colonies was to find a home with his older sister at Rothley Temple. It was to prove the turning point in his life.

Chapter Notes:

1 Following the defeat of the Catholic James II (VII of Scotland) by William of Orange at the Battle of the Boyne in 1690, the Church of Scotland was recognised as the national Church and Presbyterian as the official religion in Scotland.

2 Macaulay Journal Jan-May 1797, pp 1-12, Huntington Library, California MY465. Most historians speak of this as 'writing to a friend.' In fact they were addressed to Selina Mills whom he married in 1799 and who was clearly the only person with whom he could share these painful reminiscences of his past. It is the only recorded source of Macaulay's early life. The events are quoted extensively by his two biographers: Viscountess Knutsford (a granddaughter) *The Life and Letters of Zachary Macaulay* (London, 1900) and Charles Booth (a great grandson) *Zachary Macaulay: His part in the Movement for the Abolition of the Slave Trade and of Slavery* (London, 1934).

3 Journal, p.7.

4 Long, Edward, *History of Jamaica*, Vol.2, p.287 pp.

5 Macaulay, Zachary, *Negro Slavery or A View of Some of the more Prominent Features of that State of Society as it exists in the United States of America and in the Colonies of the West Indies especially in Jamaica* (London,1823).

6 Ramsay, James, (1733-1789) an Episcopal priest from Fraserburgh served as a naval surgeon and after an injury sustained when treating slaves on a ship, became a doctor and clergyman in St.Kitts. Planter pressure drove him out of the West Indies and he found a living in Teston, Kent in 1781 from where he provided much early evidence for the campaign.

7 Journal, p.11.

# 4

# *Is it Lawful to makes slaves of others against their will?*

Granville Sharp was of that cut of Englishman that one might call romantically eccentric. Born in 1735 at Durham, the ninth son of the Revd Dr. Thomas Sharp, Archdeacon of Northumberland and grandson of Dr Thomas Sharp, Archbishop of York, Granville was apprenticed to a draper in Tower Hill, London at the age of 15, choosing voluntarily to study Hebrew and Greek, so that he could better read the scriptures in their original form. In 1758 he obtained an appointment in the Ordnance Department, later merged into the War Office. Here he worked on supplies procured for the British Army deployed in the American Colonies.[1] An avid pamphleteer, he would rush out a text on a cause and pursue an issue or injustice by letter and by all other means. The War Office job, though tedious, only required about six hours work a day, leaving Granville time for his other activities.

Romantic in that with his brothers and sisters he would appear in colourful court garb as the core of a musical ensemble on board the King's Barge on the Thames. Granville's older brother William held the official post of Surgeon to King George III, with a grand uniform, and lived on the barge most of the year. Granville himself had a fine singing voice, and played several instruments including an 'unusual harp of his own making'.[2] On some occasions the Barge and the Ensemble were commissioned to make extensive journeys on the Thames to delight their royal patrons.

William Sharp kept an office in Mincing Lane, where each morning he would offer free medical care to the poor. One morning in 1765 Granville was just about to enter William's office when he encountered a severely battered black man also making his way to the 'King's kindly doctor'.[3] The young black man called Jonathan Strong, aged about 16 or 17, had been brought to England like thousands of other slaves by his owner, David Lisle, a Barbados lawyer. Lisle had for some reason set about Strong with the butt of his pistol, then left him in the street to fend for himself, expecting to see no more of him. As well as the swollen head from the beatings, William and Granville noted that Strong also had an ailment affecting his eyes, rendering him almost blind, which probably accounted for his brutal abandonment by his master. The two Sharps patched him up, gave him money for food & clothes, and supported him for a four and a half month period of recuperation in St Bartholemew's Hospital. When Strong was fit again, they fixed him up with a job with a pharmacist close to their office.

Two years later David Lisle spotted Strong riding as a footman on a coach used by the pharmacist's wife. With great cynicism, Lisle had the now valuable-again Strong followed home, then made a deal for £30 with a Jamaican planter for Strong. To make it stick he had Strong kidnapped and flung into jail on a trumped-up charge to await the next ship for the West Indies. Strong was able to get a letter to Granville, who tackled the issue head on. Granville first ensured that the jailer was put under no illusions as to his absolute duty 'not give him up to any person' until his hearing before the Lord Mayor. Then he informed the Lord Mayor that 'Jonathan Strong had been confined in prison without any warrant'. At the hearing the new owner brandished the bill of sale, but the Mayor discounted all objections and declared Strong free. After this Granville Sharp obtained a reputation of being the champion of blacks in London, and one of the very few people speaking out against slavery; it becoming his most important passion. Strong's putative new owner did not give up however, pursuing an action in law against William & Granville Sharp for the loss of his property rights over Strong. The case dragged on for two years during which the brothers researched the law and Granville published a stirring pamphlet: *On the Injustice and dangerous Tendency of tolerating Slavery, or even admitting the least Claim to private Property in the persons of Men, in England.* With this pamphlet in wide circulation, the plaintiffs dropped the case.

Granville Sharp's passion was now seriously engaged, arguing that the law in England did not have any idea of a person being a slave in England. This put the slave owners in a difficulty; since there were by this time several thousand blacks in this country. The experience of slaves brought over from the Caribbean to this country was of an 'exhilarating shock'. A disgruntled London magistrate wrote in 1768 about West Indian landowners bringing their slaves to Britain 'as cheap servants, having no Right to Wages; they no sooner arrive here, than they put themselves on a Footing with other servants, become intoxicated with Liberty, grow refractory, and either by Persuasion of others, or from their own Inclinations, begin to expect Wages.'[4]

As yet, there was no test case that would settle the status of slaves and slavery in England, but one soon came along in connection with an escaped slave. On 13 January 1772, Granville's diary records that 'James Somerset, a negro from Virginia, called on me this morning to complain of Mr Charles Steuart.' Somerset used the occasion of being brought to England by his owner Steuart to break with him, escape, and live a free life. Somerset was rounded up and stowed on a Jamaica-bound ship, but a court order had freed him, pending a decision in the highest Court, the King's Bench, before Lord Chief Justice Mansfield. Granville launched yet another pamphlet and sent it to the Prime Minister and all the Kings Bench judges. Mansfield approached the matter with pragmatism. He did not relish at all having to decide an issue where 'the right to property clashed with the right to liberty'. He tried to bring the parties together to negotiate their own way forward. Lawyers for Steuart argued that the property value lost if all the present thousands of Slaves in England were freed could amount to £800,000, (something like £58million today). The case dragged on for months between recesses, and became a cause celébre in the London press and prompted packed attendances at the court. Not able to get the parties to settle out of court, Mansfield handed down a judgment full of small print designed to prevent the wholesale freeing of slaves in England, merely asserting that Steuart had no right to compel his slave to go to a foreign country. Somerset was free in England, and the popular perception that slavery had indeed been outlawed in England became the prevailing mood. Henceforth 'only a handful of slaves were later ever sold or recaptured in Britain'. Granville Sharp had the judgement he wanted.

But there was another case years later in 1783. An educated and perceptive freed slave, Olaudah Equiano, brought Sharp's attention to a letter in the *Morning Chronicle* of 18 March 1783. It concerned a previous voyage of a slave ship *Zong* under Captain Luke Collingwood out of Africa with 440 slaves bound for Jamaica. As was customary, building up a full load of slaves at various points on the African coast took time, and many of the slaves would have been on board for a long time before the voyage. Unfavourable weather at sea stretched the crossing to twice its normal time, and many of the slaves were getting sick and were dying. This put pressure on the economics of the voyage, as 'dead slaves yield no profits'. Collingwood came up with a plan using the accepted norm of the shipping business, that slaves were *cargo*. If the ship's safe passage was threatened, then jettisoning cargo to save it was recognised as a basis for claiming the value of the cargo against the insurers of the voyage. The slaves were insured at £30 apiece, or nearly £2,000 in today's money. The insurable 'Peril of the Seas' the captain was going to rely on was a story that the ship was running very low on water, and that everyone on board was threatened. So he ordered his crew to throw overboard 133 of the sickest slaves, and to stick to the water story when asked in the future. Part way through this sickening episode, some of those selected rebelled, and so were put over the side with their arms still in shackles. The final ten took charge of their own destiny, and leapt voluntarily in to the sea. Miraculously one survived, clambering up a trailing rope and hiding among the remaining slaves.

The Zong's owners eventually filed an insurance claim for 132 pieces of cargo deliberately jettisoned to save the ship, at £30 each, nearly £264,000 today. In court, the insurers had the support of the Chief Mate, probably guilt ridden at the events, who testified that the ship had plenty of water, arriving in Jamaica with '420 gallons to spare, and no one having been on short rations'. The court nevertheless found for the owners, and the angry insurers appealed. Once again Lord Mansfield had to preside over a case with the keen eyed Granville Sharp taking his full interest. For Sharp had already consulted a legal expert, written his usual letters to the authorities, hired lawyers, and interviewed 'at least one member of the *Zong's* crew'. Sharp recorded in his diary that at one point, the ship owners' lawyer 'violently exclaimed to the judges that a person was in court (looking at me) who intended to bring a criminal prosecution for murder against the parties concerned: but, said he, *it would be madness: the Blacks were property*.'[5] Judge Lord Mansfield would have no truck with the idea of murder, stating that it was just 'as though horses were killed.'[6] He and his fellow judges made the decision that 'on the evidence there seems to have been no necessity for the throwing overboard of the Negroes'.[7] Mansfield ordered a new trial purely on the narrow point of whether the insurers should pay the claim.

Sharp and his informer Equiano were absolutely outraged. 132 people had been thrown alive to their deaths in the ocean, and it was not a matter for investigating a murder, merely a civil insurance dispute! Sharp turned to his pen and wrote letters all over the place to spread the news of what had happened. One such letter or its message reached Dr Peter Peckard at Cambridge in 1784, who was seriously moved by its import. Apart from preaching sermons against the trade, in 1785 as Vice Chancellor, he used the best tool in his armoury by setting a special question in the top Cambridge Latin Essay Contest: *Anne liceat invitos in servitutem dare?* --Is it lawful to make slaves of others against their will? The winner of this prize competition always gained a wide audience for the piece of work, launched by the giving of a reading before the assembled audience in the university's Senate House. Each year's winning offering would be taken up and read by the alumni of the two great universities who had themselves been schooled in the classics, and who looked forward to this annual treat.

In the year before, a 24 year old divinity student at St John's Cambridge, Thomas Clarkson, had entered a lesser Latin competition, and come out as the winner. So in 1785 he took up Peckard's question to see if he could use his Latin skills to come out top again, for the 'obtaining of literary honour',[8] never realising what he would be letting himself in for. The completed Essay had to be researched and delivered in two months, which meant that Clarkson's innate qualities of energy, hard work and persistence would be tested to the full. Clarkson read 'everything he could find', found access to a recently deceased slave merchant's papers, interviewed British officers returned from the American war, and listened attentively to his brother John, a naval lieutenant who had served on ships in the West Indies. Throughout he sought to use only first-hand testimony from those who had experience of actual slavery in operation. Clarkson won the competition, and the essay itself would have its own effect as its message spread wider. But by far the most significant effect was on Clarkson himself. In those sixty long days and nights of putting the evidence together, Clarkson found himself 'overwhelmed by horror'. 'In the daytime I was uneasy. In the night I had little rest. I sometimes never closed my eyelids for grief....I always slept with a candle in my room, that I might rise out of bed and put down such thoughts as might occur to me in the night....conceiving that no arguments of any moment should be lost in so great a cause'.[9]

That June in 1785, the Essay having been read in the Senate House, the Prize collected, his divinity studies complete and the status of Deacon obtained by ordination, Clarkson mounted his horse and headed off to a curate's post in London. The act of travelling slowly through the country-side, with little but thoughts to exercise his mind, found him running and re-running the arguments made in the Essay. 'I frequently had to persuade myself that the contents of my Essay could not be true. The more however I reflected on them, or rather upon the authorities on whom they were founded, the more I gave them credit'.[10] A crisis came as he was heading down a hill into a coaching point in Hertfordshire by the River Rib. Clarkson later wrote: 'Coming in sight of Wades Mill in Hertfordshire, I sat down disconsolate on the turf by the roadside and held my horse. Here a thought came into my mind, that if the contents of the Essay were true, it was time *some person should see these calamities to their end*'.[11]

This moment on the hill above Wades Mill would reverberate through-out the next 50 years, by which time not only the slave trade had been abolished, but even slavery itself in the British Empire brought to an end. This conclusion in Clarkson's mind, analogous to St Paul's shaft of light on the road to Damacus, became a 'landmark on the long, tortuous path to the modern conception of universal human rights'. The coming months would see Clarkson still bothered by this issue. He would retreat into the woods, the arguments in his head still raging. Steadily it dawned on him that he was the *person who should see these calamities to their end.* Translating the Essay into English was a first step, pursued reluctantly because of Clarkson's lack of confidence in his English prose skills, but his brother John helped him, and the result was an expanded, English version of his prize-winning script. A chance meeting in the street outside the Royal Exchange in London with an old Quaker friend of the family saw Clarkson and his manuscript taken to the Quaker publishing house of James Phillips, in George Yard. A deal was done, and the Essay, under the skilful editorship of Phillips, became a book, *An Essay on the Slavery and Commerce of the Human Species, particularly the African, translated from a Latin Dissertation, which was honoured with the First Prize in the University of Cambridge for the year 1785, with Additions.*

Clarkson was now not alone. His new Quaker friends saw him introduced to a new circle of books, and to people with first hand experience of slavery. Clarkson spent a month at Teston in Kent with its evangelical minister James Ramsay, who had served as a ship's doctor in the West Indies before becoming an Anglican minister on St Kitts for fourteen years. As the surgeon on board *HMS Arundel* in West Indian waters Ramsay recounted his visit to a captured French slave ship that had requested help. Dysentery was rife on the ship, and Ramsay was absolutely 'horrified by the faeces and blood that covered the slave decks'. Ramsay broke his hip soon after, resigned from the navy, and took holy orders, and for those next fourteen years 'preached to the slaves, taught them the bible in his home, and made enemies of the island's sugar planters'.[12] He was attacked by the planters, and was pleased to be offered the incumbency of Teston in Kent by the resident of Barham Court, a farm just up the hill from the church, leaving the St Kitts years behind. Living at Barham Court were Sir Charles Middleton RN, MP, later First Sea Lord in 1805, who was one of the two members of parliament regarded as an Evangelical, as was his wife Margaret.[13]

Middleton had been the captain of the ship *HMS Arundel* when Ramsay was the ship's surgeon. Lady Middleton had earlier encouraged Ramsay to write about his slavery experiences, and the subsequent essays and pamphlets when published brought down further virulent denunciations from West Indian interests in pamphlets attacking his character rather than his case.

During this month of July 1786 at Teston, a conference of similar minded people assembled, called by Sir Charles Middleton and his wife. There was Bishop Porteus of Chester, soon to be of London, a Virginian by birth and with a burning hatred of all things about the trade and slavery, as well as Benjamin la Trobe, leader of the Moravian Brethren, the only group working as missionaries among the slaves. Clarkson, helping out Ramsay in his parish, and hearing his experiences from the West Indies, was in exalted company. At dinner one day at Barham Court, Clarkson recounted his experience at Wades Mill, and then he publicly vowed to give his life to this cause, to be the *person who would see these calamities to their end*, and to do nothing else.[14] When the meeting talked about how to stop the trade and bring an end to slavery itself they ruled out simply stoking public opinion by itself. Ultimately the matter would have to be decided by Parliament. Later on, at Lady Middleton's constant insistence that her husband should call for a Parliamentary enquiry into the trade, they agreed he was not the man for this task. They settled on the name of Wilberforce, and Middleton wrote to him in Hull. Wilberforce too felt he might be unequal to the task, but promised to come over to Barham Court when next in London.[15]

In Clarkson's now ceaseless search for knowledge of the trade and slavery, he was able to board a ship the *Fly*, lying in the Thames-side docks, which regularly ran with slaves from the Gold Coast to Jamaica. 'Here I found myself for the first time on the deck of a slave vessel....the sight of the rooms below and of the gratings above....filled me with melancholy and horror. I found soon afterwards a fire of indignation burning within me.'[16] That fire and that willingness was just what a group of Quakers had been praying for. Quakers had long had experience of raising issues that went against the prevailing culture. They understood what it felt like to be outside the mainstream, because of their unwillingness to doff the cap to all authority. They were already using their networks to raise awareness of the evils of slavery, but they needed an Anglican at the front end of a proper campaign. Clarkson was their man.

Wilberforce had duly spent his time with Middleton and Ramsay, and had also met La Trobe in London. In the autumn of 1786 Wilberforce found the commuting in from Lauriston House at Wimbledon wasteful of time and money, and by Christmas he had taken up the lease of No.4 Old Palace Yard, just by the House of Lords. Early in 1787 Clarkson dropped by and left a copy of his Essay. When he called back in a few days Wilberforce 'welcomed him with open arms'.[17] The two had regular conferences, though Wilberforce had not yet fully committed himself to take the cause on in Parliament. Clarkson's Quaker friends thought Wilberforce was the ideal candidate, not just for his personal qualities, but also for his close association with Pitt, and the ardency of his new-found evangelical faith. A dubious plan was conceived to prompt a commitment by Wilberforce. Clarkson and the Quakers persuaded a Lincolnshire landowner, Bennett Langton, to stage a dinner party at which Wilberforce would be encouraged to commit himself in public. Middleton was among the guests, as well as Clarkson. Wilberforce is reported as saying that 'he had no objection to bringing the measure forward in Parliament, when he was better prepared for it, and provided no other person more proper could be found'.[18] Later early in May 1787 Wilberforce was at Pitt's home at Holwood in Kent together with Pitt's first cousin William Grenville, who would succeed as Prime Minister'. The three young men in their twenty-eighth year sat under an oak tree on the estate. Pitt challenged Wilberforce to bring forward a motion on the slave trade. The answer is not recorded, but in old age when asked why he took up abolition, he would say: 'I distinctly remember the very knoll on which I was sitting near Pitt & Grenville'.[19]

And so on 22 May 1787 twelve men assembled at the Phillips' printing shop in George Yard. Nine Quakers including the Phillips brothers and the American-born Dillwyn, and three Anglicans: Clarkson, Granville Sharp, and one other. The one-page minute of the meeting records the simple declaration: 'At a meeting held for the Purpose of taking the Slave Trade into Consideration, it was resolved that the said Trade was both impolitick and unjust'.[20] Clarkson was their man full-time 'on the road', and the task of taking on the world order began in earnest.

Chapter Notes:

1 *Clapham & the Clapham Sect*, Clapham Antiquarian Society, (1927), p.119.
2 Hochshild, Adam, *Bury the Chains*, Pan Books, (London 2005), p.42.
3 Ibid, p. 43.
4 Fielding, Sir John, *Extracts from such of the Penal Laws as Particularly Relate to the Peace & Good Order of this Metropolis* (London, 1768), pp143-145.
5 Hoare, Prince, *Memoirs of Granville Sharp, Esq.*, London: Henry Colburn, (1820), p.240.
6 Court Minutes, 21 May 1783, quoted in Hoare, p.237 .
7 Shylon, Folarin O, *Black Slaves in Britain*, London: Institute of Race Relations/Oxford University Press (1874).
8 Clarkson, Thomas, *A History of the Rise, Progress, and Accomplishment of the Abolition of the African Slave Trade by the British Parliament.* Vol.1, pp.208-209, 214-215.
9 Ibid.
10 Ibid, p.210.
11 Ibid.
12 Hochschild, p.93.
13 Pollock, p.49.
14 Ibid, p.52.
15 Trobe, Ignatious de la, *Letters to my Children*, 1851, p.22, a paraphrase, quoted in Pollock, p.53.
16 Clarkson 1, p.238.
17 Pollock, p.55.
18 Clarkson 1, p.251-255.
19 Harford, John, *Recollections of William Wilberforce*, p.139, q. Pollock, p.58.
20 Minutes, 22 May 1787, the British Library.

# 5

# *Freedom for Whites & Bondage for Slaves*

By the 18th century 'tea drinking had become a national habit, a rival to the consumption of spirits and beer; 'the cups that cheer but not inebriate' were already as well known and highly valued in the labourer's cottage as in the poet Cowper's parlour'. The tea was brought to England from the tea estates in India and China in the holds of the East India Company's ships. 'The poor sweetened the bitter herb with large quantities of sugar. Sugar from the British West Indian islands was now on every table, whereas in Shakespeare's day a very limited luxury supply had come from Mediterranean Ports'. Annual sugar consumption in England had jumped from 10,000 tons in 1700 to 150,000 tons in 1800, which even after allowing for a doubling of the population over that time, represented a per-capita increase of seven and a half times.[1]

Woven cotton brought by the East India Company to London provided a sought-after alternative to the native wool as the basis for clothing. Popular demand for cotton clothing fuelled the huge expansion of milling capacity in Lancashire. The 1801 census showed the population of Lancashire at 695,000, as against 160,000 a hundred years before. The Liverpool 'slavers' made up cargoes of finished Lancashire cotton with other goods for the trip to Africa, exchanged them for Negroes, took the slaves across the Atlantic and returned with raw cotton, as well as tobacco, sugar, and rum.[2] West Indian planters bought Lancashire cotton to clothe their workers, and the Negro labour from Africa in the American colonies and the West Indies enabled production of the raw material for the Lancashire

Mills. 'The guilty trade and innocent manufacture were mutually assistant in more ways than one.' The honest waged labour of Lancashire cotton workers was mixed together with the unfair and evil trade in raw and finished cotton of the slavers and plantation owners.

The Atlantic trade from England was shared by London with Bristol and Liverpool. French, Dutch and Portuguese slavers shared the triangular trade, but more than half the slaves made the 'middle passage' across the Atlantic shackled in the holds of British ships. In 1771 fifty-eight slavers sailed from London, twenty-three from Bristol, and one hundred and seven from Liverpool. In all 50,000 captured slaves were carried across the Atlantic that year.[3]

But this was nothing unusual in world terms. In the middle of the 18th century being a slave of, or in a similar relationship to, an owner was the lot of over half the world's population. The multiple tribes and clans in Africa would be in regular wars with one another. The victors would take their spoils, including making slaves of suitable captives. Not much is written about it, but it is felt that an equally buoyant trade in African slaves was carried on eastwards into Arab lands. Slave ship captains from England and Europe coming on the scene with holds laden with good things helped develop the mercenary spirit already abroad in the African mentality. Rounded-up Africans were exchanged for those desirable goods.

But it was a bitter business. Slaver Captains were paid a daily allowance, and a share of the profits of the voyage. There was always a trade-off between how long a Captain would cruise the coast assembling his load of slaves to get a full load, and the effect of the insufferable conditions on board leading to a high death rate, with the resultant poor profits at the slave sales in the West Indies and the Americas. The first batch of Africans to go on board into their cramped shackles might have to endure that for weeks before setting out on the seven or eight week crossing of the Atlantic. In the interests of 'efficiency and profitability' facilities to build up shiploads of slaves were progressively developed onshore. These became forts, not to keep intruders out, but to hold captured Africans hundreds at a time in chains awaiting the arrival of the ships.

That same John Newton who as the preacher had inspired Wilberforce in his youth in London, and to whom he had turned later with his crisis of faith, had been fully a part of this whole business. Newton had some colourful adventures and episodes before being given the captaincy of a slave ship working out of Liverpool. He sailed under the colours of Joseph Manesty, a successful merchant with several ships, and made three triangular voyages before suffering an injury and missing the fourth sailing. Newton kept a detailed log that 'fills 336 pages of a large leather-bound book.'[4] Whenever Newton did a deal for new additions of slaves, each one would have the initials *JM* burned onto their chest with a red hot iron to show that they now *belonged to Joseph Manesty.* Newton's log records all the horrors of the situation, the floggings, the thumbscrews, and the double chains applied to mutinous slaves and crewmen alike. Sickness would be rife, and as well as losing slaves on the passage, his ships would rarely end the triangular trip with the same number of crew as it started with. At the end of the Atlantic voyage the exhausted slaves would have to face the further humiliation of being haggled over for their future ability to labour in the plantations. Meanwhile, Newton would slip away to attend the local Anglican Church in the port.

The situation that the slaves were going to could not be more dire. If it was Jamaica they would be entering a regime where they would have to do the 'hardest manual work on earth': the cultivation of sugar cane by hand. Under a tropical sun they had to labour for twelve hours each day, planting, fertilising, and in the cutting season with backs constantly bent, brave the razor sharp edges of the cane without any covering on their hands or bodies. These bodies had also to bear the onslaught of a whole range of new diseases, which they had to fight from the weaker position of an inadequate diet. Consistent with the view that slaves were not really proper humans, the protein supplied was often in the form of salt cod left over from requirements in England or Nova Scotia, which frequently went rotten before use. This is in a Caribbean sea teaming with fresh fish. The slaves working on the American mainland had a better regime. Growing cotton was easier work, and the diet was more balanced and rounded.

For the Jamaican slaves this difference showed up in three major measures. The first was height. On average, Caribbean male slaves were three inches shorter than their American counterparts.[5] Then there was the birth rate. With many of the more skilled tasks on plantations being undertaken by men, it was the women who bore the brunt of the field work. The 'hard work, abysmal diet, delayed menarche, all brought an end to a women's fertility by her mid-thirties'. Half of all female slaves in the middle of the 18th century in the British West Indies 'never bore a child'. The third measure was life expectancy. The slaves that Newton delivered to the Caribbean could, in the words of an Antigua planter, expect to be under a policy of 'little relaxation, hard fare, and hard usage, to wear them out before they became useless and unable to do service; and then to buy new ones, to fill up their places'.[6] The mother of all sets of numbers is the chilling confirmation of how slaves in the British West Indies were 'systematically worked to an early death'. 'When slavery ended in the United States, the less than half a million imported slaves had grown into a population of almost four million'. In the British West Indies, the comparison was over two million imported against a surviving slave population of just 670,000.[7] 'The Caribbean was a slaughterhouse'.

A typical sugar plantation would have a central great house, where the owner or manager lived in ostentatious style. Ideally it would be on high ground with a view of the sea, and the occupiers would make the most of the cooling sea breezes by having their relaxing areas on verandas built on the upper floor. Sumptuous eating parties were the norm.[8] One such plantation of 710 acres located by the sea in Barbados was Codrington, for which detailed records were kept. A resident manager, not the absentee owner, lived in the great house. There were around twelve other white employees, and altogether nineteen slaves attending to their every need. In 1781 the Codrington slave headcount totalled 276 men, women and children. The inventory had the value of £70 written in as the value of the senior skilled slaves, while children's nurses were listed at £15 each.[9] The slaves had to build their own rickety shacks. Cut cane fermented very quickly, so it had to be immediately carried to the mill in huge heavy bundles and fed twice through the rollers to extract the juice. It was then treated in boiling vats and filters until being allowed to cool as the sugar crystallized. Both these mechanical processes were full of hazard; amputation of limbs and serious scalding being a regular peril. Codrington slaves worked a standard twelve hour day starting at seven am. for six days every week. 'Sundays, according to one disapproving local minister, the slaves spent in vile and viscous Practices….either in trafficking with one another, or in dancing, or in other Actions improper to mention'[10] As Hochschild observes, 'no mention of Sunday being the only time to tend their meagre vegetable patches'. Codrington slave discipline was applied with full rigour. An early measure to stop runaways was the branding on the chest, 'but in the end it was the lash, plus at some times, the iron collar and the straitjacket' that was the chief deterrent.

In a good year the Codrington books showed a profit of £2,000, around £190,000 in today's money. This bounty creamed off the backs of slavery was enjoyed by a special corner of British life, the Church of England. More specifically, Codrington's absentee owners were the *Society for the Propagation of the Gospel in Foreign Parts*, and the brand burned into the chests of its slaves had the legend SOCIETY. The Society's governing council included the 'Regius Professors of Divinity at Oxford and Cambridge and the head of the church, the Archbishop of Canterbury. It was a feature of the age, 'few people saw the contradiction between freedom for whites and bondage for slaves'.[11] Once the French Revolution erupted, merchants would promptly christen slave ships Liberté, Egalité and Fraternité. There was nothing exceptional about the Codrington ownership; the Countess of Huntingdon, leading patron of the Methodists, had a plantation. George Whitfield, the most influential Evangelical of the day, owned more than fifty slaves in Georgia and believed firmly that 'hot countries cannot be cultivated without Negroes'.[12]

This was the prevailing order that Clarkson saw as the *calamities that some person should see to their end.* Now with the London Committee in operation, and Wilberforce equally determined to play his part at the parliamentary end, Clarkson set off on his immense round of journeys to gather the evidence that would be needed to shake to the British Parliament to its roots. A Parliament made up of members elected by only one in twenty of the male population who had the vote, and who had exacted the going rate from their candidate in return for their favour.

Chapter Notes:

1 Drummond, J.C., *The Englishman's Food*, pp.242-244, quoted in Trevelyan, G. M., *English Social History*, Longmans 1945, p.387.
2 Ibid, p389.
3 Ibid, p389.
4 Martin & Spurrell, eds., *John Newton, The Journal of a Slave Trader*, (London 1962).
5 Finkelman & Miller, M*acmillan Encyclopedia of World Slavery*, (New York, 1998), vol. 2, p 613.
6 Newton's Journal 2, p.112.
7 Hochschild, p.67.
8 Ibid, p55
9 Bennett, Harry, Jnr, *Bondsmen and Bishops: Slavery and Apprenticeship on the Codrington Plantations of Barbados, 1710-1838*, California 1958, p.11.
10 Bennett, p22.
11 Hochshild, p.87.
12 Quoted in Gallay, Alan, 'The Great Sellout: George Whitfield on Slavery', p.25, in Moore and Tripp, eds., *Looking South: Chapters in the Story of an American region 1*, (New York, 1989).

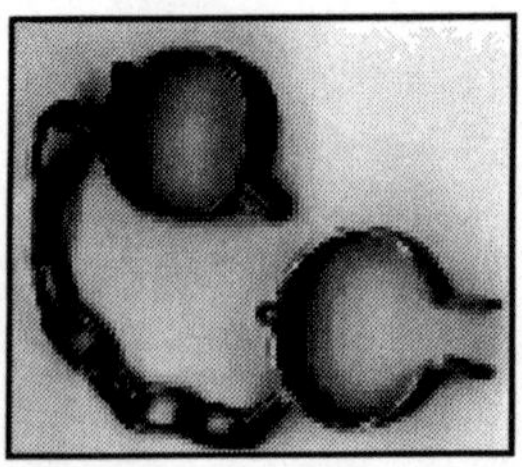

# 6

# *Fourteen Hundred Pages of Vellum*

The London Committee under the titular chairmanship of the respected Anglican veteran Granville Sharp began its work in earnest. Clarkson was dispatched with a brief to gain first hand evidence of the Trade in the port city of Bristol. This group was to employ methods that would see a whole new toolbox invented that would be a legacy to the art of campaigning in the future. They used the brilliant British stagecoach-based postal and newspaper circulation system to the full. Supporters would receive a sharply edited newsletter regularly. There was a form of direct mail, at any one time informing readers of the voting habits of their members of parliament, or urging the writing of letters to parliament, and even the time and date when an abolitionist activist would be reading from their book at the local bookshop. The reach of the London Committee would be extended by raising up local activists leading their own committees. In an age when less that one in twenty of the male population were able to vote for a representative in parliament, the Committee and its local outreach made the idea of the multi-signature petition into a most powerful weapon. When they had a good image like that of the packing-in of slaves on the regulated slave ship *Brookes*, the Committee's printing house turned them out by the thousand so that they could appear all over the land. The perceptive Josiah Wedgwood, when a later member of the committee, told his designers at Stoke to come up with a version of an idea in his mind. The resultant *Am I not a Man and a Brother* medallion became the eighteenth century precursor of the modern tee shirt slogan, or car bumper sticker, or lapel badge. It was reworked into all sorts of items like buttons and ladies' brooches, and incidentally gave women a way of participating in the campaign. The Committee members had to learn the art of lobbying parliament. Here they were at a disadvantage to the pro-slavery interests, who when the Abolitionist cause began to gain in strength, were able to use levies to fund professional lobbyists. The Committee had to rely on people who believed in the cause, and because of wealth usually from land, could give time to be in London and lend their energies.

Thomas Babington was one such amateur from the country who lent his considerable energies to the cause. On the 8 February 1788 he writes from Rothley to his wife Jean who is staying at Gisborne's home at Yoxall Lodge. By this time Jean is four-months pregnant with their first child, and he wrote thus:[1]

> 'You are, I dare say, very anxious to hear how matters proceeded at Leicester. We had not so large a meeting of County Gentlemen as at Stafford, but the town afforded us a large supply. I opened the business to about 150 people. Judging there would be no opposition I spoke for about 5 or 6 minutes. I was seconded by Dean Nichols who to my surprise happened to be in Leicestershire. He gave a particular account of the treatment of the Negroes, and, in a part of his speech where he argued against determining the point from motives of policy, he was extremely animated, introducing quotations from scripture with a force which I believe affected the whole meeting.
>
> The Petition was agreed unanimously, and Gisborne and I are to take it up to London.
>
> I told Aulay (Macaulay) not to bother with his long speech'.

So Babington here in Leicester was organising the local abolitionist committee and raising a petition. Gisborne had done the same in Stafford. Then they ride 'up to town' and find ways of making themselves useful and up to date in London.

On the 22nd February 1788 in his letter to Jean,[2] Babington and Gisborne are in London staying with the Roos family. It gives the clue how earnest these two are by how they spend their time. 'Yesterday evening we were in the House of Commons and were extremely entertained. You will see the subject of the Debate in the Paper, so I will not send it you', he writes. A little reminder here to Jean to keep up with her reading of current affairs! 'Mr Pitt was uncommonly forcible and convincing: I have never heard him more clear and strong in his argument or more happy in his language'. 'Gisborne was highly pleased with the Debate: to him it had more of novelty than to me'. Not many people today would say that sitting through debate in the gallery of the Commons was 'highly entertaining', but then we do not have the outstanding oratory of a man hardly thirty years old to marvel at. Babington continues: 'As soon as we returned here we found a note from Wilberforce inviting us to Supper. We went, and spent a very agreeable evening with him'.

This gave the three the chance to catch up on how life had moved on since those days at Cambridge, and to observe the great change that had come about in Wilberforce. On the one hand Babington wrote in awe-filled praise at the huge workload Wilberforce has taken on. As well as his large constituency post bag, Wilberforce had just launched his crusade to upgrade the nation's virtue, the popularly called Proclamation Society, as well as having pledged himself to bring the slave trade issue to parliament. Babington articulated the motives he sees in Wilberforce: 'He is continually active in some good cause which he espouses with the zeal of a man impelled, not by the fluctuating motives of vanity or ambition, but by a strong sense of duty'. Then on the other hand Babington saw his friend with his already 'delicate constitution', 'sinking under the extent of business'. Babington lays out to his wife his admiration for Wilberforce, and picked out the qualities that no doubt Babington would like to emulate:

> 'I look up to this little man with a degree of love as well as veneration. What character can be contemplated with more pleasure than that of a man surrounded by venal and ambitious politicians, but himself pure and disinterested -- with abilities which expose him to flattery,

and place high official situation within his reach, but yet remaining both independent and free from vanity, pursuing a steady and active course of duty'.

That letter was written on 22nd February 1788, referring to events on the 21st. John Pollock sets out that Wilberforce had already begun to 'sink under the extent of business' two days earlier, and on 23 February was 'forced to consult his doctors'.[3] There followed a period when Wilberforce sank very low, with a condition that through today's eyes could well have been ulcerative colitis, a stress-related illness. The doctors saved him, with a combination of unconventional prescribing and rest at Bath. But his spirits also sank into a dark place, with the weight of the coming struggle against the assembled slavery interests being a heavy burden. The prayers he entered in his notebook at Bath indicate a bleak state of mind, but the last entries show the beginnings of his recovery, where 'his prayers ask calmly for the grace to do his duty, freedom from worldly duties, from desire for applause, and from the temptation to depend on human aid alone'. On 7th May 1788 Wilberforce wrote to Pitt imploring him to take over his abolition motion in the house. He replied graciously, and on 9 May moved that 'the House should investigate the Trade'. Parliament already was doing so, since he had previously instructed the Privy Council's Standing Committee for Trade and Plantations to look at the whole area of trading with Africa. Pitt was part of the grace that Wilberforce prayed for, and no doubt those two university chums Babington and Gisborne, would at sometime be another part.

In May for a month Wilberforce lodged himself back into the quiet rhythm of life at his old college, St John's Cambridge, before hiding away at Rayrigg on Windermere for the summer with his mother and sister Sally. Meanwhile in the Commons, Sir William Dolben was steering through his Slave Limitation Bill, which paved the way for regulations aimed at civilizing the so-called 'middle passage' of slaves across the Atlantic. Wilberforce journeyed back slowly via Hull, Lincoln and Cambridge to Bath to 'complete his cure'. The slave business could not be restarted however, and neither could any other. King George III had another of his bouts of disturbance in his mind, and the parliamentary opposition wanted a Regent put in, which would have meant their side being asked to form an administration. Wilberforce, now frailer but refreshed, rejoined Pitt in the house and sat through the long hours on the Regency Committee. The House spent interminable days in February debating the Regency Bill, but suddenly and happily the King recovered, the danger slipped away, and the slave business could be contemplated again.

In the spring of 1789, after the Privy Council has produced an 850 page report, Wilberforce worked out a strategy with Pitt and speaker Grenville at Holwood, Pitt's home in Kent. Pitt proposed a series of twelve resolutions that would build into a Motion for Abolition. On 10th May Wilberforce stopped off at the Shooter's Hill home of Matthew Montagu, a parliamentary colleague who had helped him when he was very ill. There with John Ramsay, John Clarkson (Thomas Clarkson's brother) and Montagu they sharpened up the points Wilberforce would make in his speech the following day. The tactic of attempting to use twelve resolutions proved a distraction and they were never fully put. Faced with the prospect of immediate abolition, and after a nine day adjournment, the question was lost on the argument put by Lord Maitland; that for this House to 'proceed on Privy Council evidence alone would be demeaning to itself'. He held that the House should hear its own evidence at its own bar.

Wilberforce's plan that summer to go to Paris and discuss parallel abolition with the French was abandoned after the news of the fall of the Bastille on 14th July. Thomas Clarkson picked up the baton, and went instead, to stir up the French abolitionists. No one knew this presaged the full-scale Revolution. Wilberforce spent the summer interval touring country houses from Bath to Buxton to Norfolk, including a two week spell at Gisborne's house at Yoxall. When the house resumed in January 1790 Wilberforce used a successful tactic to have the whole-house committee changed into a Select Committee meeting separately. This set him an arduous task, since with William Smith, the Member for Sudbury, who had a house at Clapham, they spent months organizing the hearing of evidence. The pro-slavers finished by April, and by June the evidence amounted to several thousand pages, only to be brought to a halt by Pitt's sudden decision to call a General Election. Wilberforce scuttled up to Yorkshire, but such was the nature of the opposition and the success of the canvassing that he and Duncombe were returned 'without the expense of a poll'.

After the election Wilberforce collected his mother from Hull and they joined Henry Thornton, the London banker, fellow Evangelical and Member for Southwark, at the summer residence being used by the Sykes family in Buxton. The confirmed bachelor Thornton met the Sykes' daughter Marianne, who he later would marry. Wilberforce, his mother, and Marianne then headed off to Gisborne's Yoxall Lodge, deep in the Needwood forest. Already at Yoxall were Thomas and Jean Babington, ready for what had been arranged as a heavy working summer. The Babington, Gisborne and Wilberforce team set to work on the evidence given to the Select Committee on behalf of the petitioners against the Slave Trade. The evidence of the pro-slavers had been completed and digested back in April; the task before them now was to prepare the rebuttal, digesting and consolidating the statements of all the witnesses against the Trade. One thrust of the pro-slavery interests was that 'Slavery was mild, the Middle Passage comfortable, and the Blacks were worse off in Africa'. Captain Thomas Wilson, R.N., of HMS *Racehorse*, in his submission, 'epitomized the Abolitionist evidence': 'It is a Trade evidently founded on injustice and treachery, manifestly carried on by oppression and cruelty, and not infrequently terminating in murder'.[4]

The three worked upstairs under great pressure of time to create a digest ready for publishing. Marianne Sykes described the activity in a letter to her mother:[5]

> '...they have never appeared downstairs lately except to take a hasty dinner, and for an hour after we have supped. The Slave Trade has occupied them for nine hours daily. Mr Babington told me last night that he has 14 hundred folio pages to read to detect the contradictions and to collect the answers which corroborate Mr Wilberforce's assertions in his speeches.....the two friends begin to look very ill, but

they are in excellent spirits and at this moment I can hear them laughing at some absurd questions in the examinations proposed by a friend of Mr Wilberforce's. Every corner of this house is crammed with books, and people are free to read or go out or come in and do exactly as they like. I have left Mr Babington reading to Mr Wilberforce in the corner of the room. Mr Gisborne correcting the proof sheets of his book in another, and Mrs Babington, Mrs Gisborne and I have been 'discussing' in the middle of it. We all have supper at eight o'clock and a little after nine wonder that we should sit up so late, and retire to our rooms'.

Here the St John's Cambridge team is seen at its best. Babington and Gisborne had worked hard at their undergraduate studies, gaining mastery in the Classics as a precursor to Babington's Law qualification, and Gisborne his Divinity studies. Gisborne was becoming an accomplished writer and poet. Here they would have been very close to the heart of the Abolitionist case, becoming well-attuned to helping Wilberforce draw out of the evidence the heads of his future speeches. They would also have been much in tune with each other as troopers in that small but growing band of Evangelicals coming to be known as the 'Saints', the so called Clapham 'Sect'. The 'Sect' would later address many social issues of the day, including encouraging thrift, sound education, prison reform, proper respect for people regardless of station, generally aimed at increasing the sum total of human happiness. The Abolition of the Slave Trade would be their really significant involvement, alongside the founding of the Bible Society so that the Scriptures could eventually be read in every tongue.

The resultant summaries of distilled evidence would be added to in 1791, and made into a 648-page report.[6] Eventually, at the request of the London Committee, Thomas Clarkson would further distill the material to a quarter of its size. This *Abstract of the Evidence....* would become a huge best seller, finding its way all over the land and into the British Caribbean. Even now the crisp, clear, statements, unembroiled by biblical references, are chilling to read. Here is one passage:[7]

> 'When [slaves] are flogged on the wharves....they are described by H Ross, Morley, Jeffrys, Town, and captain Scott, to have their *arms* tied to the *hooks of the crane*, and *weights of fifty-six* pounds applied to their *feet.* In this situation the crane is wound up, so that it lifts them nearly from the ground and keeps them in a stretched posture, when the whip or cowskin is used. After this they are again whipped, but with *ebony bushes*, (which are more prickly than the thorn bushes in this country) in order to *let out the congealed blood*'.

But to reach the goal of the Abolitionists' struggle, even with the growing massive clamour from evidence and petitions all around the country, and unrest in the slave plantations overseas, a majority of the vested interests of the House of Commons had to be achieved. Moreover, it had to be achieved in such a way and manner that would leave the unrepresentative Upper House no option but to endorse the will of the elected house. For Wilberforce the burden of leading this effort in Parliament was monumental, only made easier by his sense of duty and calling, the help of the many activists and colleagues, and the presence at key times of his two chums from Cambridge days, Babington and Gisborne.

Chapter Notes:

1 TB at Rothley to JB at Yoxall, Babington MSS , box 13.4.
2 TB in London to JB at Yoxall, 13.14.
3 Pollock, p.79.
4 In *Abstract of the Evidence.....before a Select Committee...1790 and 1791*, printed by James Phillips, London 1791, p.50.
5 quoted in Pollock, p103. Marianne's letters to her mother are in the Thornton MSS 7674 held in the library of Cambridge University.
6 Hochschild, p.196.
7 *Abstract of the Evidence*, quoted in Pollock, p.71.

*The* **Zong** *incident. One of the many cartoon-style representations of the throwing overboard of 133 sick and ailing slaves en-route to the West Indies. The resultant court ruling that no murder was done, because it was 'just as if horses were killed', so enraged Granville Sharp that he wrote the letter to Dr Peckard at Cambridge that led to Thomas Clarkson winning the famous essay competition.*

*Drawing by Frank Besse of leg shackles recovered archaeologically from a sunken slave ship.*

*The Henrietta Marie transported about 200 slaves from the Bight of Biafra to Jamaica.*

*Courtesy of David Moore, North Carolina Maritime Museum.*

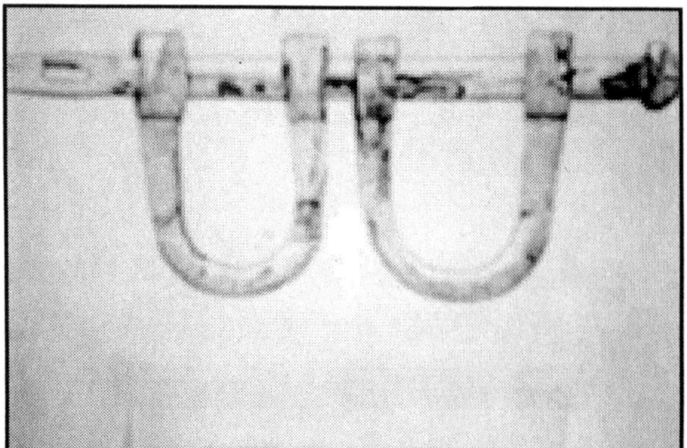

**William Wilberforce** *(1759-1833) aged 29. Image from the portrait (oil on canvas) by John Rising (1753-1817).*

***Thomas Babington** (1758-1837). Image from the portrait by C E Wagstaff, mezzotint (after J Hoppner).* 

**Yoxall Lodge**, *the Gisborne family home deep in the Needwood Forest, near Burton on Trent.*
*A Photograph from the beginning of the 20th Century with kind permission of The Magic Attic, Swadlincote.*
*The Lodge is now demolished, but the land is still unspoilt and is farmed by a family who open it each year to enable people to walk the bluebell trails.*

# 7

# *A New Start at Rothley Temple*

Zachary Macaulay arrived at Rothley Temple from Jamaica in the winter of 1789. His granddaughter was later to describe the experience for him as 'overpowering and bewildering.' It was a shock to the system of those in Rothley. One of Thomas and Jean Babington's daughters recalled that her uncle Zachary was thought by people locally to be 'a disagreeable, conceited youth, with self-sufficient dogmatic manners' and that he did not commend himself to anyone.[1] The arrogance born of the colonial mentality and given expression by the insecurity of a new situation was hardly surprising. Although it was tempered by the influence of the Babingtons, it would be many years before it was replaced by a genuine humility and an ability to work creatively with different allies.

His older brother-in-law, as well as providing shelter and hospitality, offered counsel, guidance and advice. Thomas Babington saw through the younger man, but he gained his confidence as no one else could have done. Relating his early life to his then fiancée Zachary was to write 'With Babington I have been in the habit of using still less reserve than with any other of my friends. This circumstance makes it probable that he knows me in some respects better than I know myself.' He made it clear that it was Babington's acquainting her with his character that gave him the courage to unleash the painful story of his past. No one else at this time could have turned the key of freedom in the life of a deeply inhibited and up to now unloved and unlovely young man. In the same way he attributed the awakening of his religious conviction to his older brother-in-law, by example as much as by doctrine. 'What an amiable man is Babington,' he wrote in 1797 'surely there are few souls on which the lineaments of the divine character are more fairly and more deeply drawn.'[2]

Anyone living at Rothley Temple in the last decade of the eighteenth century would have to be in hibernation not to be aware of the importance of the abolition of the slave trade to those who made visits there. The 1788 campaign of petitioning had forced Parliament to institute the enquiry into the trade. Evidence was flowing into the Privy Council. Abolition committees all over Britain were seeking those who could support their work with the first hand experience which Wilberforce, Gisborne, Babington and Clarkson did not have. The young Thomas Clarkson, on leaving James Ramsay's rectory in 1786, had told his mentor that he was eager 'that I might begin my labours (in anti-slavery); according to the pledge I had given him.'[3] It would be some time before Babington's oversight of Zachary Macaulay at Rothley was to bear the same fruit, but the parallel is not too far fetched.

At Rothley Zachary encountered for the first time some of the band of men who were to be known in history as 'The Saints,' later 'The Clapham Sect.' They did not, as earlier historians have implied, bring about the abolition of slavery single handed. Nevertheless even one of their strongest critics, the Caribbean premier and historian Eric Williams, described them as 'a brilliant band.'[4] They were generally wealthy and privileged, but in two respects they presented a radical challenge to the establishment. They were united in the conviction that Christianity needed to be freed from the shackles of a state religion where lip service was paid to public respectability regardless of belief, obligations, or moral behaviour. That conviction led them to seek to right what Zachary Macaulay would later describe as 'the violation of every acknowledged principle of the religion of Christ;' the trafficking and enslavement of fellow human beings.[5]

It was to be nearly another decade before Zachary Macaulay was to join Wilberforce, Clarkson and Stephen actively in the cause. These ten years were to be formative and traumatic for the young Scot; far more so than his baptism of fire in Jamaica. They were to be years which took him into the heart of the slave trade, whilst being the agent of those dedicated to its destruction. They were to be years too in which love, an emotion with which he had been so unfamiliar, burst on the scene for him and developed into as life-long a commitment as the cause to which he was to give so much of his life. Thomas Babington was once again to provide the trigger for the next stage in Zachary's life thousands of miles away.

The now veteran abolitionist Granville Sharp had realised, from his encounters with Jonathan Strong, the extent of the black population of London, estimated at one point in the eighteenth century to reach 15,000. Sharp sought to give as many as possible a new start in life and started a scheme to purchase land for settlement in Sierra Leone on the West African coast. His vision was of a black-led colony that would be a model of freedom. Sharp's motives were pure, but there was more than a hint of ethnic cleansing by those who saw the scheme as an opportunity to get rid of unwanted London black residents. The first attempt at a settlement proved to be a failure for various reasons, but in 1791, with parliamentary approval, the Sierra Leone Company was set up with Henry Thornton, a wealthy banker and distant cousin of Wilberforce, as its first Chairman. Thomas Babington was amongst the Directors.

Zachary Macaulay had not secured employment since his return from Jamaica and his brother-in-law suggested a trial period in Sierra Leone. In November 1790 he set off on *The Lapwing* in company with Rev. Nathaniel Gilbert, newly appointed Chaplain to the Colony whose companionship, according to his granddaughter, was thought by Babington to 'prove beneficial to the religious training of his mind.'[6] Thomas Babington and his friend Henry Thornton saw this also as a wider training for the young man whose previous experience might enable him both to adapt to the punishing climate of West Africa and to meet the challenges that Sierra Leone posed. It was to prove more of a cauldron than they could imagine.

Early in 1792 twelve hundred former slaves, who had joined the British forces in the American War of Independence and landed in Nova Scotia, arrived in Sierra Leone. They were led by John Clarkson, a Lieutenant in the Royal Navy and brother of Thomas. The Company had appointed him in place of the charismatic former slave Thomas Peters, acknowledged leader of the Nova Scotia black community, who had already travelled to England to inform Sharp of the 'betrayal' of the British government's promises of land and freedom. The Company's concern to keep control of Sierra Leone in white hands flew in the face of Sharp's vision and had already caused opposition from Equiano and his black colleagues to the project. This policy, as others, was to dog Zachary Macaulay's time in the colony.

In contrast to his Jamaican experience, Zachary found himself in congenial company within the small circle of administrators sent out from Britain. He obviously impressed them since the Directors appointed him Deputy to the Governor of Sierra Leone, an appointment he took up in January 1793 after some months back in England. A Swedish botanist employed by the company noted: 'Mr. Macaulay, the second in Council, who arrived lately, is a very clever and sensible man, an elegant writer of great application, and besides of the same turn of mind as Mr. Dawes.' Governor William Dawes suffered badly from ill health and when he returned home in March 1794, Zachary Macaulay, at the age of twenty-six succeeded him.

The Company's view of the colony had moved away from Granville Sharp's original vision of an autonomous self-governing community of ex-slaves. Henry Peters and his colleagues felt, with some justification, that the Company's control over judicial and religious power and the access to resources left the settlers very much second class citizens. Over the years the Governor found himself defending a structure that was not of his making and in circumstances where diplomatic relationships with the surrounding kings and chiefs, some of whom were slave traders, were for ever in need of careful handling. On top of that, the colony was dependant on slaving vessels for supplies and communications. Co-operation with Bance Island, one of the biggest slave stations on the coast, was necessary for survival. The Company was deeply unhappy about this, but saw Sierra Leone as a witness at the heart of the trade. Therefore when Assistant Governor Macaulay in July 1793 returned five slaves who had run away from Richard Horrocks, a slave trader at the Isles de Los station, they were as horrified as the settlers were angry.[7]

In a sense the incident highlighted how much the colony was between a rock and a hard place. Zachary pointed out in his report to the Thorntons that slave trading was not only legal but if the traders took drastic action to recover their 'property,' the Company risked revenge kidnapping and the enslavement of freemen. He stated that he had no powers to emancipate and if the Company's servants violated British law they would be abandoned by it. A member of the Board wrote 'no' in the report's margin and those who shared Sharp's ideals must have been sorely tried. No reprimand was issued to the Assistant Governor, but for the rest of his time in Sierra Leone the incident rankled with him, and in every similar instance he found ways to avoid any more handing over of runaway slaves.

Macaulay had himself exchanged membership of one national Church for another and in his time only clergy of the Church of Scotland and the Church of England were permitted to solemnise weddings and act as official chaplains to the colony. Naturally the Methodist and Baptist missionaries resented such restrictions and two of the latter, Messrs. Garvin and Grigg, encouraged their people to challenge both the chaplains and the Governor, refusing to cooperate with them. In seeking to act as a go-between, Zachary's inexperience led him to some tactless and high handed judgements, but he would have needed the Wisdom of Solomon to have avoided these disputes.

Only six months after he became Governor, the colony was attacked and invaded by the revolutionary French navy in September 1794. Many of the Company's buildings were sacked and looted, and although the sailors mainly targeted these, the settlers' homes were not left alone. Zachary went on board the flagship and seems to have reached an accommodation with the French commodore but observed that the Frenchman had no means of imposing discipline. Nonetheless some provisions were secured and many of the settlers' homes saved from burning. Most of the Company's servants lost their homes and were accommodated by settlers. Zachary freely acknowledged this debt and the kindness shown towards those who were regarded, and regarded themselves, as the rulers.

Soon however, the question of returning to the Company materials salvaged from the French broke this uneasy cordiality. One good thing, he noted, had emerged from the invasion. 'The destruction of the Isles de Los and Bance Island and the capture of almost all the slave-ships on the coast,' he wrote, 'have given a severe blow to the Slave Trade, and notwithstanding the Company's losses, have brightened their prospects.'[8]

Zachary's health had suffered severely with the strain of the job and the punishing West African climate. He needed home leave and took it via the West Indies in April of that year. He travelled on the *Ann Philippa* a ship carrying 225 slaves to Jamaica via Barbados. He stopped off at Barbados and kept notes on slave conditions in a personal diary written in Greek letters as a possible code. These notes were later to be of great value in the campaigns with which he would become increasingly involved.[9]

When he arrived back to Britain, the Babingtons' had taken a house in Sidmouth, to enable the improvement of Jean's health in the sea air. Zachary was disappointed not to be at Rothley but travelled frequently to London to see Wilberforce and Thornton, who quickly introduced him to their friend Hannah More, the celebrated poet, dramatist and philanthropist. The More sisters ran a number of schools around Bristol and one of the teachers, Selina Mills, had become almost a member of their family. Despite the attempts of the sisters to prevent the possibility of a romantic attachment with a young man returning to the unsuitable company and climate of West Africa, Zachary was totally smitten with Selina and her with him. To the More sisters' horror, the two came to 'an understanding' days before he sailed.

The next three years saw the development of this love affair at a distance. A year after he arrived back Zachary wrote to Selina 'your letters have increased my esteem and affection for you in a degree which beforehand would not readily have been conceived. They have helped also I am sure to humble me and to soften down a few of the asperities of my rugged nature.'[10] In lengthy journals and letters he poured out his heart, relating his early life and frankly sharing with her the tensions with settlers, missionaries, local chiefs and traders. Unusually for that era, he engaged her in theological and political questions, taking her opinions very seriously. This was a prelude to his enthusiasm for women sharing in anti-slavery activity, an idea which horrified Wilberforce.

Selina Mills enabled Zachary to break free of so much that had inhibited him. Six months after his arrival back in Sierra Leone he sent her a lock of his hair and requested a cameo of her. When it arrived he wore it round his neck but was not pleased that the artist had tried to improve on her features, and wrote: 'I am half angry with him for thinking you required any exercise of his creative fancy.' That same month he acquired a parrot, which only spoke Fulani. Zachary planned to teach it to tell Selina constantly how much he loved her, and put it on a ship bound for Bristol, but the bird died before he could put the plan into action.[11]

Zachary Macaulay's commitment to the anti-slavery cause had never been in doubt, despite the Horrocks affair. He inherited a tangled situation in Sierra Leone which he did not always handle well. He held the colonial and missionary assumptions of his day and as Governor his concern for discipline could verge onto the side of cruelty. But against strong social pressure he showed considerable leniency towards an early rebellion by the settlers and it was under his auspices that a black jury was to condemn to exile a white malefactor, an incident that led him later to be vilified in the press at home. When he left Sierra Leone finally in April 1799, he did not sail alone, but in company with three dozen African children, selected to be educated with a view to their future return as missionaries. Looking after their needs, giving evidence on the slave trade to the House of Lords, and recovering from intermittent bouts of fever took up most of his first days back in Britain. This meant that his communication with Selina was by letter and even then he was tormented with guilt for failing to communicate daily with her.

The couple were married in Bristol at the end of August 1799, and after an obligatory visit to the More sisters, they spent their first few weeks together at Rothley. Through the Thorntons they secured a house in Lambeth. Zachary started work as Secretary to the Sierra Leone Company. Soon after the New Year in 1800 Selina became pregnant and for the last three months of her confinement, Zachary left her in the hands of the Babingtons. Their first child was born, in what is now Room 10, at Rothley Court Hotel on 25 October and baptised Thomas Babington Macaulay a month later, the name indicating all too well the close family ties.

For a man as genuinely modest as Zachary, being father of a son destined for great things cannot have been easy. Tom's genius from an early age charmed Hannah More, who became his favourite 'aunt' and held him in adulation. Yet early letters to school and Trinity College, Cambridge, indicate a father's stern concern, not just to ensure the right company and moral influences, but for prompt replies to his letters and application to studies. It was a special relationship, but held particularly Scottish characteristics. Tom's independence of spirit was strongly mixed with a desire to please his father, and none more so than in his speech to the Anti-Slavery Society in June 1824 with the Duke of Gloucester in the chair. Wilberforce, Stephen and Henry Brougham, the Edinburgh lawyer and politician were all ecstatic. The *Edinburgh Review* described it as 'a display of eloquence so signal…from one who for the first time addressed a public assembly.' Zachary, bursting with pride but concerned not to show it, simply asked his son Henry 'Was he too long?' When they returned home his only comment to Tom was to remind him that a young man should not speak with folded arms in the presence of royalty.[12]

Chapter Notes:

1 Knutsford, p.15. The Babington daughters' comments were made to Margaret Holland, Viscountess Knutsford, who was a cousin.
2 Zachary Macaulay to Selina Mills, 4 Feb 1797, Huntingdon Library. San Marino, California.
3 Clarkson Vol.1., pp.203-30.
4 Williams, *Capitalism and Slavery*, (London, 1944).
5 Macaulay, *Negro Slavery*, p.118.
6 Knutsford, *Life and Letters*, p.20.
7 Macaulay, *Journal*, 3 Aug 1793, Huntingdon Library.
8 Macaulay, *Journal*, 26 Nov 1794, Huntingdon Library.
9 Macaulay, *Diary*, May 1795. The diaries from 1794-1799 are in the possession of descendants and will be deposited in time in the library of Trinity College, Cambridge.

10 Zachary Macaulay to Selina Mills, 4 Feb 1797, Huntingdon Library.

11 Ibid.

12 Trevelyan, G.O., pp.103-5.

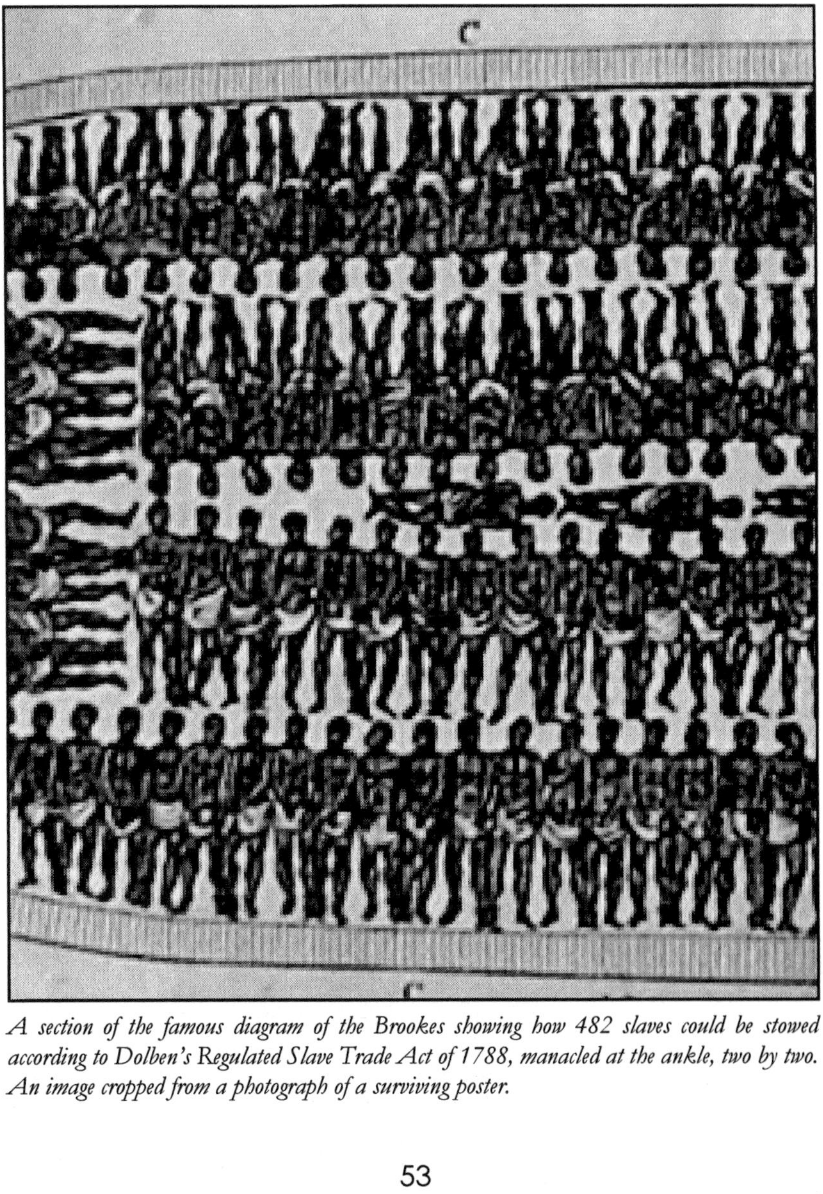

*A section of the famous diagram of the Brookes showing how 482 slaves could be stowed according to Dolben's Regulated Slave Trade Act of 1788, manacled at the ankle, two by two. An image cropped from a photograph of a surviving poster.*

**Old Palace Yard, Westminster.** *Wilberforce took a lease on No. 4 in December 1786 to have a base right next to Parliament. Babington and Gisborne were to be regularly in residence here at Wilberforce's right hand at crucial moments in the abolition campaign. From a drawing by Canalletti and etched by J. T. Smith. By courtesy of the Dean & Chapter of Westminster.*

# 8

# *The Path to Gradual Abolition*

At the end of 1790 the Select Committee returned to evidence gathering. Thomas Clarkson, who had worked so assiduously and travelled many hundred of miles to recruit witnesses, went on the road again. He was particularly anxious to find one person who had served on a ship with his brother John. Clarkson boarded '317 ships, some three quarters of the Royal Navy, and to his 'inexpressible joy' found his man and returned to London with him and five other witnesses'.[1] This witness was able to give testimony that would refute the oft repeated pro-slavery response that 'they acquired their cargo only from black dealers, buying people who were already slaves in Africa'. The witness would describe how the crews of British slaver ships in heavily armed canoes would cruise the Niger Delta kidnapping Africans for the Trade.

After the evidence gathering had ended early in 1791, there was a further big editing job to be done, this time quickly in London. The London Committee provided activists for this, including a new recruit, William Dickson. A Scot, born in Moffat, Dumfrieshire, Dickson had been Secretary to the Governor of Barbados. He would later take a commission from the London Committee, and from Wilberforce, to Scotland, and there take on the mantle and travelling style of Thomas Clarkson, north of the border. Thomas Babington came up to London from Rothley in April, this time with his brother Matthew, the Vicar of Rothley.[2] They would have been alongside Wilberforce at Old Palace Yard as Wilberforce arranged the heads of his speech for the debate that started on 18th April 1791. On the other side of the cause there was a new member in the Commons, elected in the 1790 intake for the slaver port of Liverpool. Banastre Tarleton was the fourth of seven children born to the ship owner and slave trader, John Tarleton of Liverpool (1719–1773), who was a mayor of Liverpool in 1768. Tarleton did not complete his studies at University College Oxford, joining the British army instead. As a young man, he had inherited £5,000 on his father's death, but squandered it all on gambling. In 1775 he purchased a commission as a cavalry officer in the 1st Dragoon Guards, and proved to be a gifted horseman and leader of troops. He was often championed as a hero for his startling successes for the British in the American War of Independence, but acquired an unenviable reputation for brutal treatment of the colonists.

In the Commons, Tarleton spoke on military matters and a variety of other subjects, but especially the slave trade, with which the port of Liverpool was particularly associated. In reality, Tarleton was working to preserve the slavery business of his brothers Clayton and Thomas, and he became well-known for his taunting and mockery of the abolitionists. This reputation started in the 1791 debate, when according to the notes prepared by Sir William Dolben, the speaker of the Commons: 'Tarleton's arguments are that the Trade is sanctioned by Parliament and that they could not give it up without break of faith; the value of the Trade; and then digressed into a downright vulgar scold of the Ministers .... that the men who would destroy the Trade are fanatic dreamers'.[3] Another supporter of the Trade, a Grosvenor uncle of Lord Belgrave, was noted by Dolben as arguing that the 'Trade was nasty but necessary, and the wisest thing we can do is to shut our eyes, stop our ears, and run away from the horrid sounds without enquiring about it'.

Speaker Dolben made notes after reading The Senator's version of Wilberforce's four hour speech and they reveal a reasoned and revealing judgment on the justice and humanity of the matter before the house:[4]

> 'His preface is such as I should think would lay fast hold on the attention of every man who had ears to hear, and a heart to feel. His

clear, circumstantial and plain account of this dreadful business, with the vouchers he produces in proof of his aspersions are sufficient to baffle all contradiction, and the whole of his strong arguments are urged with a peculiar gentleness and modesty'.

Just after 3.30am on 20 April 1791, with Thomas and Matthew Babington watching from the Gallery, the House divided. Only half the members were present, and sadly the vote was Noes 163, Ayes 88, a majority against the Abolition of 75. Drake of Shardiloes had predicted the vote, saying that 'the Leaders were for the Abolition, but the minor orators, the dwarfs, the pygmies, would this day carry the question against them'.[5]

This was the summer when the Sierra Leone Company was being formally constituted which detained Wilberforce and Babington in London. Wilberforce had left Pitt's at Holwood on 2 August to be in London to tidy up the arrangements, and in a letter to Elliot, Wilberforce wrote:[6] '…and am somewhat uncomfortably dangling about this hot town--in two or three days I expect to be released from this obligation to stay and shall bend my course for a very short visit to Cookson [in Norfolk] …. and then sit down for *good* at Babington's in Leicestershire'. By 8 August Wilberforce was at Rothley Temple, writing letters, especially to John Clarkson, about to set out on the voyage to collect the freed slaves in Nova Scotia for the adventure of joining the settlement in Sierra Leone. That summer in Rothley was the time to draw breath, to re-consider the tactics to follow in the 1792 session of Parliament, and to romp around the park with the children. Babington and Wilberforce, and no doubt with others who might have dropped by, would all have contributed to the discussions, and the play.

Meanwhile, Thomas Clarkson, ever hopeful, left behind a very dispirited London Committee and climbed back on his horse. Everywhere he went there was the new phenomenon of the consumer boycott taking place. Indignant at the spurning of Abolition by Parliament, people up and down the land were giving up the use of sugar from the West Indies. The idea partly came to many people from reading specially produced pamphlets, like the one that featured a 'dialogue between a Negro and an English Gentleman, selling an estimated seventy thousand copies in four months:[7]

> *Mr English.* Why Cushoo, what's the matter?
> *C*: Ah! Massa, poor Negro worse usé den dog.
> *E*: What have I to do with that, Cushoo, I'm no planter.
> *C*: But you drinké Rum and Sugar, Massa.'

There even sprang up a version of today's 'fairtrade' products. Sugar from India was actively sold by some grocers as being produced by the 'labour of FREEMEN'.[8] Clarkson was also very active in promoting the distribution of his pocket-sized *Abstract of the Evidence*. It was being read everywhere. Copies even reached slaves in the West Indies, which stoked the ire of the planters, and added to the climate of incipient slave revolt that had to be frequently suppressed.

But late in August a 'volcano' erupted on the French plantation island of St. Dominique, the modern Haiti, once dubbed by Pitt 'the Eden of the Western world'.[9] While Wilberforce and Babington watched the children playing by the Rothley Brook, and talked of tactics to achieve that elusive majority in the British House of Commons, an army of the enslaved and of free mulattos on St Dominique rose up and put hundreds of French whites to the sword. This was no ordinary rebellion; it became a full-scale war, producing the legendary figure of Toussaint L'Ouverture as the leader of the slave forces. It was ferocious, brutal on both sides, and accompanied by the wholesale destruction of large parts of the economic capacity of the island. Twice as big as Jamaica, and very productive, St Dominique had been responsible for thirty percent of sugar exports from the West Indies. In spite of all attempts by the French, and the British for a time in the Anglo-French conflict, and then Napolean's forces later, the colony was never subdued, and in 1804 declared itself to be self-governing Haiti, the first Black state in the West Indies.

Those early ripples in 1791 and 1792 reverberated around the West Indies and Britain. Back in London in December 1791 Wilberforce wrote to his friend Cookson that his 'chief plan' lay in 'mobilizing the virtue and humanity of the people'.[10] He intended to give notice of a fresh abolition

Motion just after Parliament convened at the end of January 1792, sending a signal for the 'commencement of action to all our numerous and widely dispersed friends'.[11] Pitt had counselled against such an earlier move in the previous session, fearing that Wilberforce's cause would be damaged. The revolutionary fervour across the channel was in full swing. The St Dominique rebellion had added to the upward drift in the price of sugar which reached new highs. 'British Caribbean planters were rushing new land into production', and the number of ships committed to the Slave Trade showed that Britain was 'in the midst of its peak year of traffic' to date, 'with an average of three or four ships leaving British ports for Africa every week'. The West Indian interest spent liberally on its own lobbying campaign, bringing out its own books and pamphlets painting a rosy and comfortable picture of slave life.

Wilberforce pressed on with his intentions, and the petitions flooded in from all over the country. The one from Edinburgh, observed in the making by the new young emissary to Scotland, William Dickson, was so long that it 'stretched the whole length of the Commons floor'. Parliament was inundated with over 500 petitions in a matter of weeks, and the total number of signatures was over 390,000. 'In some small towns, almost every literate citizen had signed'.[12] In March Thomas Babington came up from Rothley and joined the team at Old Palace Yard. While Babington was in London, his wife Jean migrated to Gisborne's home at Yoxall with her three children Thomas (3+), Lydia (2), and John, nearly 1. Matthew was due in September, and this pooling of childcare with Mary Gisborne was a good response to the absent fathers. These lines from Babington's letters at Old Palace Yard to Jean at Yoxall give a feel for the activity of those weeks in the Spring of 1792.[13]

10 March: 'Wilberforce is not in the house, and I hear he intends to go to Clapham. Whether he will change his plan, and take me with him, I do not know'.

12 March: 'Wilberforce thinks his Slave Trade Business in a good way. The number of petitions which come up every day make a

considerable impression in the minds of the members. Mr Clarkson knows (he says) of 182 places which either have petitioned or are about doing so. The interference of the People is so *extremely* important in this affair that I am extremely glad that we and Gisborne have taken such pains and even that he was, so he says, *taken in* to go to Derby. I wish I could have met him there'.

17 March 'Escaped both cough and cold. Investigating the horrid affair emerging from a trial between a Slave Captain and his Sailors. Lord Muncaster breakfasted with me this morning'. 'Today I dine in Old Palace Yard. A young Physician who is going to Sierra Leone will be one of the party'.

19 March '…heard Mr. Pitt twice yesterday [from the Commons Gallery]....dined with Mr Thornton…this morning breakfasted with Grant [a member of the East India Company]'.

21 March 'Wilberforce is, I fancy, going to take his papers to Holwood or Shooters Hill where he may be quiet, and consider Slave Trade business well. I shall know more when I see him. This plan will, I fear, break my engagements with Mr S Thornton on Friday, and Sir C Hudson on Saturday. I have just read the evidence delivered at the trial respecting the Slave Ship, and I find it to the full to be as strong as I expected from the original presentation of the case.'

22 March 'We have just heard this moment that Denmark has abolished the Slave Trade. This is excellent news both on account of the *immediate* effect it will produce, and as an example to other nations. Gisborne arrived safely here yesterday. The Slave Trade debate will come on April 2nd instead of March 29th'.

At Clapham

23 March 'Staying at William Smith's, and dining today at the Thornton's. The West Indians seem to be seriously alarmed by the petitions which pour up every day, and by the determination which seems to exist in so great a part of the community to leave off West Indian produce. I fear however we cannot hope to see the Trade abolished at present'.

At Old Palace Yard

26 March 'Wilberforce becomes more and more busy as the time for his motion approaches, and our engagements keep pace with his'.

27 March '....scarcely a moment'

'....am very busy writing my thoughts for Wilberforce on a particular view of his question....I got no walk either yesterday or today, but intend to go out this afternoon if I can'.

28 March 'I am still extremely busy. Last night I sat up till past twelve writing a letter for the Morning Chronicle on the subject of the Slave Trade. Today I must go and vote as a Proprietor of the Sierra Leone Company. Afterwards I shall try and get into the gallery of the House of Commons. Poor Gisborne is a poor deal plagued with a pain in his face, and prevented from going out. He talks of having a tooth drawn if it continues'.

'Petitions pour in. Yesterday 63 were presented. We had a petition from Cardross, Bonhill and another parish yesterday'. [Cardross in Scotland was Jean's home].

29 March 'Busy as ever. This morning I have been employed for 3 hours examining the Mate of a vessel which with 5 others

> fired their cannon for four or six hours on an African town last August, because the natives would not sell the slaves as cheap as the Captain's wishes. Many were killed, all fled that could. The houses were built of reeds and were no sort of defence'.

These accounts of activity show how the 'Cambridge team' of Babington & Gisborne pitched in behind Wilberforce at the crucial moments. No doubt they would have helped to keep him calm and focused, and been ready foils for Wilberforce to try out ideas for his speeches. Unlike today's political staff teams, or 'policy units', these 18th century 'staffers' gave of their time, energy and resources freely. There was no monetary gain for them. Their only reward the satisfaction that what they were doing was right in terms of *justice*, *humanity* and *sound policy*.

When on 2nd April 1792 the debate came in the Commons, the public gallery was packed to overflowing, and the assemblage included Equiano, the one-time slave who had tipped off Granville Sharp about the *Zong* court case. Banastre Tarleton, the member for Liverpool, set about Wilberforce's measured contribution with a series of falsehoods about humanity in the middle passage. Against the background of the fervour of feeling in the country for abolition on the one hand, and the uncertainties of revolution and rebellion abroad, Henry Dundas, the Home Secretary, joined the debate. Up until now, no one knew where he stood. The effect of his speech, and the 'not now but later' amendment he proposed, allowed the 'timid majority exactly what it needed: a way to end a divisive national controversy, to look enlightened and respond to popular will, and to make no immediate changes'.[14] In spite of a brilliant speech by Pitt as the early morning light began to herald a new day, the House voted for *Gradual* Abolition of the Slave Trade by 230 votes to 85. It was a blow for the Abolitionists. Gradual might turn out to mean *never*. Babington wrote to his wife at Yoxall:

> 'We sat till 6 o'clock in the gallery of the House'. ....'*Gradual* Abolition is decided on but what is best is a

> full confession on the part of a very great majority of the House that the Trade is a *system of Crimes* etc, and that it has seen its death's wound and cannot long stand'.

The House broke briefly for Easter and resumed the debate on regulations and the meaning of *gradual.* Babington had gone home but was back in London writing letters again on 23 April. Various fixed dates were proposed and discounted before the business foundered on its movement to the House of Lords, who wanted neither gradual nor immediate abolition. The Lords decreed that they would have their own examination, which process was 'monopolized by the slaver interests until Parliament adjourned for the year'. The whole campaign went cold. Abolition Committees stopped meeting. A dark period ensued.

Babington left town for Yoxall Lodge on 1st May to be with his wife and children. In his letter he says 'I intend to sleep at the Temple on Wednesday night, and to ride to the Lodge on Thursday. We shall I hope leave the Lodge early the following week, for I wish to be at home in order to receive my rents and attend to other business'.[15]

Chapter Notes:

---

1 Clarkson, Vol.2, p.177.

2 TB at Old Palace Yard to Jean B at Yoxall, 21 Apr 1791, Babington MSS.

3 Dolben MSS at Nothampton Record Office, D(F) 59.

4 Ibid.

5 Pollock, p108.

6 Wilberforce to Elliot, 2 Aug 1791, Stanhope MSS, Kent Record Office, 731 (11).

7 Hochschild, p.192.

8 *The Diary, or: Woodfall's Register*, 27 December 1791, quoted in Hochschild, p.194.

9 Guoted in Martin Ros, *Night of Fire: The Black Napolean and the battle for Haiti*, (New York: Sarpedon, 1994), p.55.

10 Wilberforce to Cookson, 30 Dec 1791, Lewis-Walpole Library MSS, Farmington, Connecticut.

11 Ibid.

12 Drescher, Seymour, *British Mobilization in Comparative Perspective*, OUP, (New York, 1987), 1, p.82.

13 Babington MSS, Trinity College, box 13, 30-53.

14 Hochschild, P.233.

*The address panel from Thomas Babington's letter of Twelfth December 1788 from his base at William Wilberforce's house, to Mrs Thomas Babington at Rothley. Babington MSS at Trinity Cambridge, Box 13.17.*

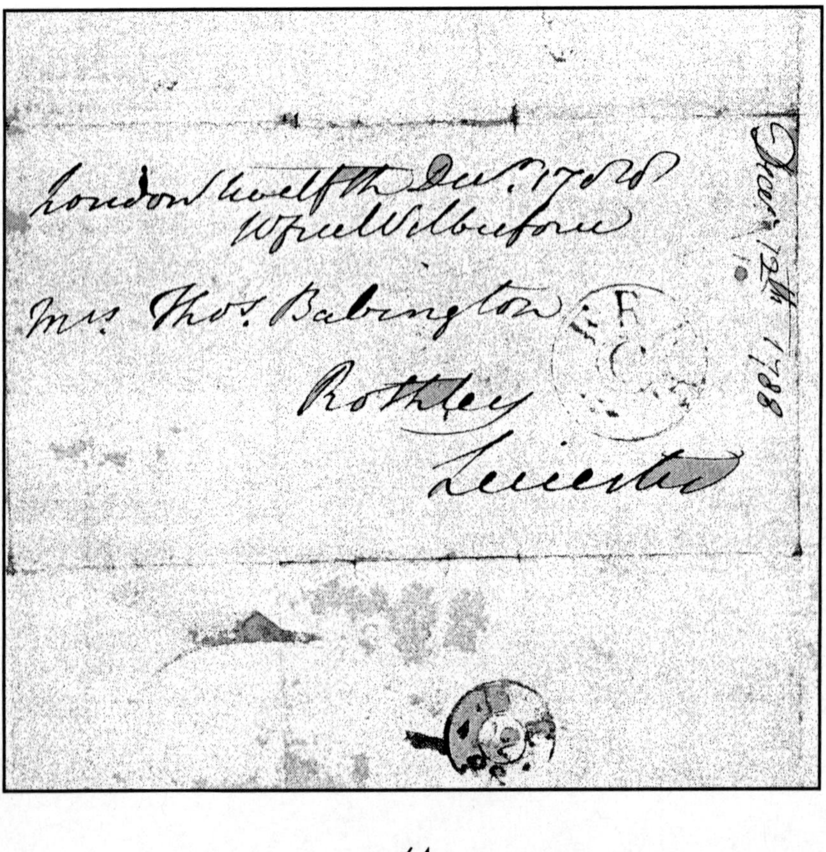

# 9

# *Lightened by Love*

Early in 1792 Henry Thornton bought a large house and estate on Clapham Common called Battersea Rise. He built two other houses on the estate, Broomfield and Glenelg. Pitt's brother-in-law the Hon. Edward Elliott took on the first, and Charles Grant, the Scottish East Indiaman, the other. Wilberforce and Thornton were cousins, and when suggested, Wilberforce took up Thornton's offer and joined him at Battersea Rise in a sort of 'chummery', sharing both the stimulus of agreeable company, and the working expenses of the housekeeping. Wilberforce kept on the lease of his Parliamentary base at Old Palace Yard.

At the same time in 1792 the Rector of the local church at Clapham died, and by the terms of Thornton's father's will, the post was in the end offered to the 33 yr old John Venn. Venn had served his curacy there several years before, where he made a serious impression. As well as lighting up the consciences and sensibilities of the many rich people of the area, Venn attended to the needs of the poor. He instituted a district visiting scheme, so that no one would slip through the net of care, and brought in Sunday evening worship, so that the poorer people, who could not be free to attend in the morning, could come to worship and receive instruction.[1]

The library at Battersea Rise became the debating chamber of the more radical group of Evangelicals that came to be labelled the 'saints', or the 'Clapham Sect'. Holy Trinity Clapham under John Venn became their point of celebration. Babington would be a frequent visitor. Other prominent 'members' set up home nearby. They occupied themselves with the other issues close to their heart, including the eventual foundation of the Church Missionary Society and the British & Foreign Bible Society.

The sense of togetherness and identity among this group was a strength in the years of the 1790's, after the declaration of war with France in 1793. With the Abolition debate disappearing into the fog of the House of Lords, and the army of France gathering on the other side of the channel, the country generally became a more repressive place. The fear of revolution saw clampdowns on popular dissent and on big gatherings. Political life became subservient to fighting the war, which took on its bloodiest form in the West Indies, after France unilaterally declared all the slaves in its territories free in 1794. The British Army was putting down insurrections everywhere across the Caribbean. The drain on its force of soldiers was immense, and the strategy of recruiting local natives, as in India, was quietly adopted. The Army resorted to purchasing slaves straight off the boats from Africa, at '£60 or £70 each'. Some 13,400 slaves were purchased over time for army service, sanctioned by Pitt's cabinet, which may account for his becoming more lukewarm on abolition.[2]

For several years Wilberforce put up various Abolition Bills, but even the ones that staggered through thin houses, went on to simply 'fall asleep' in the Lords. Wilberforce's arch opponent in the Commons, Banastre Tarleton, had an ally and counterpart in the House of Lords in his friend the Duke of Clarence, third son of King George III. The two 'were part of a high-living set who bet heavily on horse races, prizefights, and once a ten mile race between a flock of turkeys and a flock of geese (the geese won, costing the Prince of Wales £500').[3] For his apprenticeship he was enrolled in the Royal Navy, and in the West Indies developed the high-living and dissolute lifestyle that was to be his trademark. Lacking other frames of reference, Clarence quickly absorbed the mindset of the plantation owners. In his maiden speech before the assembled Lords, Clarence 'called himself an attentive observer of the state of the negroes who found them well cared for and in a state of humble happiness'[4]. He was a devotee of the widely held view in the country that the 'health of the navy, the merchant fleet and the

Caribbean colonies all rested on the Slave Trade; remove that one vital link and the empire was gone'.[5]

It was with this mindset in the Lords that the fate of Abolition Bills was being decided. In 1799, the Lords were still having hearings of witnesses. In late May of that year Babington was on hand in London, sitting in for the campaign observing the proceedings in the Lords. Zachary Macaulay, now back from Sierra Leone, wrote to his fiancée Selina Mills at Bristol on 1st June, from Battersea Rise:[6]

> 'Yesterday I was obliged against my will to omit writing. I thought my examination [appearance before the Lord's Committee] might have come on, and there was much still to prepare. I purposed indeed to have written to you from Mr. Wilberforce's house in town, but on getting there I found the House of Lords already assembled, and our attendance of course requisite. The whole evening was consumed in examining our adversaries' witnesses, who were very ably cross-examined by Lord Grenville. Their evidence was very paltry, and indicating strongly a determination of making everything they said, if possible, bend to their interests. When I first appeared before their Lordships, the Duke of Clarence was pleased to distinguish me by several significant nods. Babington stood next to him for some time and found him extremely warm against the Bill. It is shocking that such a young man, under no bias of interest, should be so earnest for the continuation of the Slave Trade, and especially now its horrors are confessed by all'.

But there were other things stirring in this very dry season for abolition. Thomas Clarkson, who had continued to carry before him the challenge arising from his Cambridge essay, had initially stumbled after the compromised 1792 vote for gradual abolition. For a period in 1793 the effects of his non-stop peripatetic lifestyle and his intensive emotional engagement overtook him. He endured a rash of symptoms that Hochschild suggests we would today call a nervous breakdown. Clarkson became disaffected with organized religion, and resolved to cease wearing his black clerical garb. He moved into a period of retirement, bought himself a plot of land in the Lake District on which he had local help building his first ever house, becoming a successful mixed arable and livestock farmer. More than that, Clarkson grew seriously close to the daughter of a family friend, Catherine Buck, who had helped him for several years with the endless copying of texts that his journeys produced. They were married in 1796, and the union was blessed with a son ten months later. They moved in the same circle as Wordsworth and Coleridge, and Clarkson used this time to carry out his own writing project, a massive three volume history of the Quakers in Britain.

Perhaps this yearning to be close to another, and not alone, was catching. Henry Thornton, the rich banker and house sharer with Wilberforce at Battersea Rise, asked Marianne Sykes for her hand in marriage. Marianne, present at that marathon editing session at Yoxall in 1790, was not sure about accepting. She consulted both Wilberforce and Babington before responding, and they were married in February 1796.[7] This caused the inevitable changes to the chummery at Battersea Rise, Wilberforce moving out so as not to disturb Thornton's new-found connubial bliss. In that winter of 1786/7 Wilberforce started having second thoughts about his presumption of a bachelor life. In a later 1821 letter to Lord Calthorpe, Wilberforce would recall that he had begun to wish 'not to finish my journey alone'.[8] In Bath that summer with Babington, who had taken a house there, Wilberforce confessed this sentiment. For such a man as Wilberforce, at 38, finding the right person was a tall order. Wilberforce's 'extreme vivacity and rapidity of thought and action certainly require no small firmness of nerve',[9] Zachary Macaulay had observed, commenting earlier on whether Marianne Sykes would have been right for him.

Babington knew the Spooner family of Elmdon Hall, near Birmingham, with a second house at Bath. Isaac Spooner, a wealthy banker, merchant and ironmaster, had a 20 yr-old daughter Barbara who had recently eschewed the round of balls and assemblies and adopted a new evangelical Christian faith. It looks as though Babington engineered a wheeze where Barbara, a keen arms-length fan of Wilberforce, wrote to him asking for some spiritual advice. On the 13th April the charmed Wilberforce discussed her letter with Babington. Two days later Wilberforce met Barbara and was totally smitten immediately. Babington knew how to look after his friend. The courtship proceeded apace, but before the quiet wedding at Walcot near Bath on 30 May 1797, Wilberforce's literary labours of the past few years came to fruition. He had long hoped for a way to explain his faith and the biblical basis on which it stood. He had been battling away at assembling the 491 pages for a long time. One summer at Yoxall, Mary Gisborne had acted as his scribe, pulling together his dictated notes and the jottings he had scattered all over the house. His *A PRACTICAL VIEW of the Prevailing Religious system of Professed Christians, in the Higher and Middle Classes in this Country, contrasted with Real Christianity* was published on 12 April 1797, and became a best seller, and a long time classic. Elliott, the owner of Brookfield at Clapham, died soon after the marriage, and Wilberforce purchased it from the executors as his new family home. Barbara's rather protective concern for him may well have induced Wilberforce to ease his schedule, and to spend more time at home, probably the best prescription he could have had for prolonging his life.

We have already heard how Babington and Jean were closely involved in Zachary Macaulay's transmission to the married state with Selina Mills in 1799, and how it was to Rothley Temple that the couple came for the birth of their first child in 1800. In the space of less than five years, four of the key players in our story, Thornton, Wilberforce, Macaulay and Clarkson, all having their days lightened by married love. In that same year of 1800 there was a by-election for the two members of Parliament for the Borough of Leicester. Babington carried off one seat, the other going to Samuel Smith, of the banking family of Wilford, Nottingham. Babington now joined the swelling band of 'Clapham Saints' in the house, who faced an increasingly complex political climate for their hopes of abolition.

The bitter, brutal and devastating war on St Dominique was now soaking up the lives of Napoleon's best troops. Even though the native leader Toussaint L'Ouverture had been captured by a deception, and much of his officer corps shipped away to captivity, huge numbers of French soldiers succumbed to tropical diseases. On 1st January 1804, the victorious slaves and mulattos threw off the yoke completely and brought the independent nation of Haiti into being. Napoleon's twenty-two month campaign to regain France's jewel in the Caribbean cost the lives of 'more than 50,000 soldiers', more casualties than he would suffer at Waterloo' in 1815.[10] Only the strong British military presence kept the lid on the slave populations of the British possessions, but the perceptions were changing. Lady Nugent, the ever observant wife of the Jamaican Governor, wrote in her journal that whenever her dinner guests discussed the new nation, the 'blackies in attendance seem so much interested, that they hardly change a plate, or do anything but listen. How very imprudent, and what *must* it all lead to!'[11]

One side effect of the war with France was the stance which other nations took, particularly America, whose ships and trade were officially *neutral.* Whereas the Royal Navy by the end of 1805 had virtually cleared the Atlantic of French, Dutch and Spanish ships, their colonies were still able to thrive by the use of *neutral* ships. American ports were often used as transshipment or just ship re-flagging points, so that neutral 'American' ships could then cross the Atlantic with plantation output to France, unmolested by the Royal Navy.

Enter James Stephen. As a younger man in London he had a very complicated love life and after gaining a qualification in law he took off to Barbados in 1783, where he judged there would be greater earning potential away from his London affairs. Very soon after his arrival some friends told him about a murder trial that was about to begin, which was popularly thought to be biased against the four accused slaves. Stephen sat in on the trial. The owner of two of the accused slaves refused to pay a lawyer for their defence, and the judge publicly applauded that stance, to Stephen's utter amazement. The evidence against the accused was very thin, and a terrified slave girl witness seemed to say what she was instructed to say. Stephen believed that the four accused were innocent, and was appalled to hear of the death sentence that was meted out to two of them. They were *roasted alive!* This incident was to shape his whole practice on the island, and when much later in London as an internationally respected authority on maritime law, he would be of particular assistance to the abolitionist cause.

In 1805, James Stephen wrote a long pamphlet about this called *The War in Disguise*. It argued that Britain had the right to strangle this trade in neutral ships that benefited its enemies. Stephen knew the 'well-concealed secret that many, possibly the majority of the supposedly neutral *American* slave ships were in fact owned by Britons, manned by British crews, and outfitted in Liverpool, flying the American flag of convenience'.[12]

Stephen's *anonymous* book had been widely read, and by March 1806, it had created an understanding that activity which supported hostile colonies gave aid and succour to His Majesty's enemies. That month Stephen called on Wilberforce at Old Palace Yard and suggested a radical alternative to putting up yet another Abolition Bill. His plan was to put up a short Bill confirming an earlier ministerial *Order in Council* banning the re-export of slaves to conquered Dutch Guiana, and 'quietly attach to it all the provisions of the oft-defeated Foreign Slave Bill'.[13] These provisions were: Slaves shall not be imported into captured colonies; no ship trading to foreign territories shall be fitted out in Britain or British colonies; no British capital or labour shall be used for such slaving. Once into law, this measure had the potential to cut a huge swathe out of the British Slave Trade

Wilberforce quickly saw that no general Abolition Bill should appear anywhere near it, and went immediately to the new Parliamentary Ministry of Fox and Grenville, who took the plan on board immediately. Stephen was retained by the Law Officers to help draft the Bill, which went through all its stages in both houses by mid-May. Hardly anybody was alive to its unstated abolitionist agenda, being glad to assent to measures that would hurt Britain's enemies. Banastre Tarleton read the runes however, 'fuming helplessly in the Commons that the abolitionists were now coming in by a sidewind on the planters'.[14] The Duke of Clarence, in the upper house, protested that the 'bill would yield the British trade to foreigners who would not use them with such tenderness and care'.[15]

The abolitionists now felt the fresh wind. The Committees started up again. A motion of intent to bring in a comprehensive abolition measure launched by Fox in the Commons and Grenville in the Lords was carried by both houses. The Trade became an issue in that summer's General Election, and the subsequent 'Ministry of All the Talents' led a new Parliament now containing ex-military men who had first-hand recent experience of the slave economies and the cost of making them work. The London Committee rented 16 Downing Street as campaign headquarters, putting maximum effort into lobbying members of Parliament. Learning from the difficulties of the past, where Bills launched in the Commons came too late to the Lords for adequate time to be given before Parliament rose, Grenville launched his Abolition Bill in the Lords in January 1807. In his speech launching the second reading at the beginning of February, Grenville put more emphasis on the preamble's 'for sound policy' reasons rather than on those of 'justice and humanity'. The debate went right through the night until at 5am the peers voted overwhelmingly for Abolition, 100 to 36. The Committee stage cleared the next evening.

On 23 February the Commons assembled for its great debate on the second reading of the Grenville-Howick Bill for Abolition. The tide was clearly flowing in the abolitionist cause, six members standing up hoping to be called as each speaker sat down. 'The climax came as Solicitor-General Romilly, who loved Wilberforce not only for Abolition, but for his interest in penal reform and the poor, swept the house to a pitch of excitement by his peroration. He contrasted Bonaparte and Wilberforce each retiring for their night's rest; Bonaparte in pomp and power at the summit of ambition, yet with sleep tormented by the blood he had spilt, and the oppressions he had committed. And Wilberforce, returning after the vote that night into the 'bosom of his happy and delighted family, to lie down in pure and perfect felicity conscious of having preserved so many millions of his fellow creatures'.[16]

'The House rose almost to a Man and turned towards Wilberforce in a burst of Parliamentary cheers. Suddenly above the roar of hear hear, and quite out of order, three hurrahs echoed and echoed while he sat, head bowed, tears streaming down his face.' Later, when the house divided, the Ayes totaled 283, the Noes 16. Before the Bill became law, strengthened by upgrading the penalty clauses from a mere misdemeanour to a crime, Wilberforce however had to give up one his cherished aims. Fearing a hostile reaction to the third reading, Howick 'took out of the Bill's Preamble the wounding words, 'contrary to *justice* and *humanity*, leaving only *sound policy*'. But the Duke of Norfolk declared that abolition was the 'most humane and merciful Act passed by any Legislature in the world'.[17] And Wilberforce's faithful aide Babington witnessed it all, this time not from the gallery, but in the Ayes voting lobby, and among the massed voices of 'hear, hear'.

Chapter Notes:

---

1 *Clapham and the Clapham Sect*, p.101

2 Buckley, Roger N., *Slaves in Redcoats: The British West India Regiments, 1795-1815,* Newhaven, Yale U.P.

3 Hochschild, p.185.

4 *Parliamentary History*, T.C. Hansard, 1814.

5 Hochschild, p.187.

6 Knutsford, *Life & Letters*, p.220-221

7 Marianne Sykes to Joseph Sykes, n.d., Thornton MSS 7674 L10.

8 Wilberforce to Lord Calthorpe, Dec. 1821, Calthorpe MSS.

9 Knutsford, *Life & Letters*, p.204.

10 Auguste & Auguste, *L'Expedition Leclerc 1801-1803*, Port au Prince, Haiti, 1985, quoted in Hochschild p.294.

11 Maria Nugent, *Lady Nugent's Journal of her residence in Jamaica from 1801 to 1805, ed.* Philip Wright, Kingston: Institute of Jamaica, 1966, p198 (4 Mar 1804).

12 Hochschild, p.303.

13 Pollock, p.201.

14 *Parliamentary Debates from the Year 1803.....*, T.C. Hansard 1812, Series 1, Vol.6, col.919.

15 *Ibid*, Vol.7, col.228.

16 *Ibid,* Vol.8, col.978.

17 Davis, David, *The Problem of Slavery in the Age of Revolution....*, (Ithaca New York, 1975), p.449.

When Freedom first in England rear'd its head,
And o'er the land its grateful blessings spread,
All hearts united, swore to hail its Laws,
And Leicester stood the foremost in the cause,
The Senate fill'd by men of Freedom's choise,
The Nation flourish'd under Freedom's voice.

Ye Men of Leicester, now assert your rights
And crush that Despot, who for Slav'ry fights;
This M— — —ra, this poor orphan's foe,
This Irish Cath'lic, this known friend to woe;
This is the Man, who tears from Afric's shore,
The wretched Negro, to return no more,
This is the Planter, this the lord of slaves,
Thro' him the orphan weeps, the widow raves.
Yes! this is he, who stands in freedom's cause,
The friend of slavery, and Cath'lic laws,
His galling whip besmears the Negro's back,
His voice is *cheering*, but his heart is black.

Can Britons hail, can Britons guide that hand,
That brings dishonour on their native Land?
Can Le'ster Freemen aid a tyrant's sneer,
When Men like SMITH and BABINGTON are here?
All friends of Freedom, as a thing of coarse,
Admires the great, the noble Wilberforce,
These are his friends, the one by kindred ty'd,
When slav'ry vanish'd, both stood near his side,
These are the Men oppos'd by slav'ry's voice,
These are the Men that claim a FREEMAN'S CHOICE.

*An Election Poster circulating in April and May 1807 when Samuel Smith and Thomas Babington were seeking re-election for the two seats of the Borough of Leicester.*

*Held in the Leicestershire County Record Office at reference Misc 15/70, used with permission.*

# 10

# *'Look it up in Macaulay' The Anti-Slavery years*

On 18 January 1823 the editor of the *Imperial Magazine* received a letter which read; 'Mr. Macaulay presents his respectful compliments to the author of an excellent paper on West Indian slavery signed "Observer." He would feel himself particularly indebted to the author if he would afford him an opportunity of personal communication, as the subject is one which deeply interests him.'[1]

That note symbolises the commitment of Zachary Macaulay to the cause to which he was to devote much of his life. So much of his work since returning from Sierra Leone had been administrative. After the abolition of the slave trade, the Sierra Leone Company became The African Institution, committed, in the language and ideas of the time, 'to promote the civilisation of Africa.' Zachary was its Secretary until 1812, combining this with his business enterprise and with a third job - editor of the *Christian Observer*. This was the organ of the Clapham Sect, but with a much wider influence. Wilberforce was once heard to say that God had set two great objects before him - 'the suppression of the slave trade and the reformation of manners'(morals) The *Observer* followed this theme, taking up issues of theology, morality and religious enthusiasm, but abolition had a prominent place in its columns.

Charles Booth claimed that Zachary Macaulay was the only 'Saint' whom the Duke of Wellington liked. He represented the abolitionists at the long peace negotiations of the Congress of Vienna and impressed Wellington, now Ambassador to Paris, with the scope of his statistics, and his fluency in

French. Even after Britain had abolished the trade, the ending of the war with France meant that lobbying was needed to ensure that their slave trade should not be restarted. It took until 1819 to secure this, but Wilberforce spoke to Macaulay of the weight 'with which your zeal, diligence, and method of preserving your papers have loaded the scale in our favour.'[2]

Some years later in the 1820's, when the campaign to abolish slavery itself was gathering momentum, Wilberforce acknowledged this meticulous fact gathering by remarking 'let us look it up in Macaulay.'[3] Zachary was a founder member of the campaign established in early 1823 For *The Mitigation and Gradual Abolition of Slavery*, which, as with the earlier one against the slave trade, promoted the cause through local committees and petitions to Parliament. Two years later he founded *The Anti-Slavery Reporter*. This became not only the main source of information or ammunition for the Parliamentary campaign, but a regular means of communication with individuals and committees sympathetic to the cause. Within a few years, its circulation rose to 20,000. Macaulay avoided polemic and simply presented the facts from original sources, which he ferreted out day and night. In 1826 and 1830 he reproduced advertisements in the *Royal Jamaica Gazette*, indicating slaves for sale by the marks on their backs and mutilation of their bodies. 'We will not cease' he wrote 'to call the attention of our countrymen to these abominations, as long as they are suffered to exist.'

There is a good Scots maxim 'facts are chiels that winna' ding.' Such watertight evidence threatened West Indian interests and drew the strongest fire from them and their mouthpiece, the newspaper *John Bull*. Zachary was mocked as 'Saint Zachariah' and 'Zaccarine' after his support for a boycott of West Indian sugar. The paper was outraged at his having used a black jury to convict white men in the colony and accused him of illegal profiteering in Sierra Leone. 'We will never quit the subject,' it thundered, 'until we have torn the veil [of hypocrisy] asunder and displayed the system of Macaulayism to the broad glare of day.'[4]

Zachary instituted libel proceedings against *John Bull* but in the light of the advice from his friends, relinquished what would have been a very long drawn out process. There were more vital concerns, such as the abolition of slavery.

Sadly, poor health and the sudden death of Selina in 1831 weighed him down too much to enjoy the triumph of 1833. It did not lessen the work he did for the cause. When others flagged, he encouraged James Stephen in a letter written only two days after Selina's death, with the words; 'Defeat I regard not. Let us do our duty, and leave the issue to Him who ordereth all events.'[5]

By the late 1820s the business enterprise in Sierra Leone which had been entrusted to his incompetent nephew Thomas Gisborne Babington and his extravagant cousin Kenneth Macaulay, had collapsed. For the rest of his life Zachary Macaulay lived under financial hardship, dependant on his children for support. Typically he faced this with the same acceptance, seeing it within God's providence, though at another level it would have been a terrible blow to his pride.

This stoicism and attention to duty have led many historians to portray Zachary as a stern unbending self righteous fanatic, awkward in personal relationships, a cold and withdrawn figure, more at home with facts and figures than with people. His family biographers have tended to present him, at least in his adult life, as a paragon of piety and humble virtue, and impeccable in his judgements and dealings with others in the cause of God and humanity. Neither tells the full picture.

It is not easy to assess the man and his achievements in between these contrasting judgements. The nearest English equivalent to the Scots word 'thrawn' is 'stubborn' but it doesn't entirely cover that native quality which enabled Zachary to stick to his task when others were falling away. That task could be coping with the French invaders or slave traders in Sierra Leone or withstanding the attacks of the West Indians in Parliament. He could make unreasonable demands on others and be intolerant at their disagreements with him or their failures. His sense of duty led him to make sacrifices of his health through overwork, or of time with his family through frequent absence. In one of the many love letters to Selina he confessed how much he was plagued with guilt over his neglect of her. There was something of the Calvinist work ethic, when he confessed to Selina; 'You cannot think what a dissipated afternoon Babington and I spent together yesterday,' as he described how they went to see a conjuror, rope dancers and gas light experiments instead of being at their desks.[6]

Rothley and the Babingtons gave Zachary Macaulay a home to which he frequently returned to find warmth and acceptance. There the transformation began, of an arrogant young man from the colonies into a self effacement, which tended to mask his prodigious contribution to the anti-slavery cause. It was there that he found it possible to love individuals and to find an individual whom he could love, trust and honour. It was there that he found a faith in God that relied more on compassion than fear, whom to follow meant a wider sense of humanity rather than a narrow tribal allegiance of race or church. This did not mean that he avoided rash conflicts, nor that he quickly abandoned prejudices against a variety of people. It did not prevent some serious ill judgements and, even worse, dignifying these with the will of God! But in the end his greater sense of his own frailty than that of others informed his devotions and kept him human.

Towards the end of his life Zachary Macaulay lived in Paris with his youngest son Charles. Through a friend at the British Embassy a seat was obtained at the Opera and one evening the old man rather shyly asked his son if he might use it. Charles was apprehensive about what his father, who had never been to a theatre, would think about such a performance. Next morning at breakfast Zachary looked at his son and said gravely; 'Charles, these are marvellous men'. So was he.

Chapter Notes:

1 Letter in private hands.
2 Knutsford, *Life and Letters*, p.315.
3 *Dictionary of National Biography*, Vol.22, p.419.
4 *John Bull*, 28 Nov 1825.
5 Zachary Macaulay to James Stephen, 31 May 1831, Huntingdon Library.
6 Zachary Macaulay to Selina Macaulay, 4 July 1807, Huntingdon Library.

# 11

# *The Unstoppable Tides*

The tides ebb and flow, and at certain times of the year, are either higher or lower. From time to time they are backed up by mighty winds, which might wreak havoc on the shoreline. All the time, the shore wears away, or is displaced and remade somewhere else. So it is with the affairs of men and nations, and also with the heart that beats in a man. At the time of the abolition victory in 1807 Babington was almost 49, and Wilberforce 48, well into middle age. The depredations of philanthropy on Wilberforce's modest fortune required him to lower his costs, so in 1808 with Barbara and the children he bought a house at Kensington Gore, overlooking Hyde Park and generally semi-rural. Today the Royal Albert Hall sits on the site. Broomfield out at Clapham was sold, and the remaining lease on Old Palace Yard was bought by Henry Thornton, who kept it available for Wilberforce when he was too late or tired to walk home from Parliament. The white-flecked waves of reputation flowed over Wilberforce, and he was dubbed the 'Arbiter of England'. His opinion and support were frequently sought, and he continued to give informal leadership to the group of 'Clapham saints' in the House. In 1812 his ailing capacity for the immense workload that his Yorkshire Constituency entailed led him to resign the seat, and he then sat for the borough of Bramber, an arrangement brokered by his wife's cousin, Calthorpe.

A strong spring tide arose in Wilberforce and the 'Saints' with the legislation to renew the charter of the East India Company when it came up in 1813. Until now, India had been closed to those who would spread the Christian faith, and there was reasonable evidence that some of the practices of Hinduism were against justice and humanity. A clause had been drawn up for the charter renewal Bill providing for the establishment of an Anglican Bishopric in Calcutta, with several archdeaconries. That clause came to be debated on 22nd June 1813 which saw Wilberforce rising to a full Commons and for three hours lighting up the house with his eloquent and glowing 'language of the heart'.[1] The subsequent flow of Christian missionaries into the Indian sub-continent was perhaps the life work dearest to Wilberforce's heart. In 1815 the war with France ended, and pressure was placed on the peace negotiators to secure the end of the Slave Trade. In 1817 Spain signed a treaty to end the North Atlantic Slave Trade. Then in 1817 the British Parliament brought in the Slave Registration Bill, which forced planters in the colonies to provide a biennial list of their slaves. Outside Parliament there was as yet no co-ordinating group raising public pressure for emancipation. In 1825 Wilberforce himself retired, to a small estate at Mill Hill, there to help his son William develop a farming and retail dairy business. The leadership of the emancipation struggle in Parliament had passed to Thomas Fowell Buxton, a social reformer inspired by the Quakers, who sat as MP for Weymouth until 1837.

Thomas Babington meanwhile had been developing a banking business in partnership with John Mansfield, an official of the Leicester Corporation. Babington split his half share of the profits with his son Matthew, who did most of Babington's detailed arranging.[2] He probably was schooled in the idea by his fellow MP for Leicester, Samuel Smith, whose family owned Smith's Bank in Nottingham, an eventual building block of the National Westminster Bank. In the General Election of 1818 Babington switched allegiances and initially put his name up for the County, instead of the Corporation, but thought better of it and stepped out of politics into retirement with his family and estate at Rothley Temple. Now at age 60, Babington turned to putting his energy into improving his estate, working with his tenants and making judicious purchases. His still-visible contribution was the extensive planting of oak trees in the Park in front of the Temple, and the carriageway he laid out from the turnpike to the house, avoiding the town. A lodge was built on the turnpike entrance, and the route lined with trees. It crossed the Rothley Brook by a new brick bridge that still bears the datestone 1819. He and Jean had fitted in making ten children in his mostly London-based career, and the Temple was a very happy place for them. His second son John was Rector of nearby Cossington.

Whilst Babington was in the calmer waters of his home port, the swirling wind of change blew up into a storm in the Caribbean. In 1823 a Slave revolt in Demerara was put down with great brutality by the British Army, and an English missionary, John Smith, was made a scapegoat and sentenced to death. 250 Slaves died. It seemed a new tide was building, and in the same year a new society was born in London, albeit with great 'timidity'.[3] The London Society for Mitigating and Gradually Abolishing the State of Slavery Throughout the British Dominions did not at the outset invite the 63-yr old Thomas Clarkson, but his friend William Allen wrote his name onto the Committee. In two trips within a year, Clarkson rode a further 10,000 miles up and down the land, making way for the new tide, which saw 230 branches set up and 777 petitions delivered to Parliament.

But *gradual* emancipation was seen as but a ripple in a pool to many people. Elizabeth Heyrick, a Leicester widow funded by her wool merchant father, had brought out a storming pamphlet, *Immediate not Gradual Abolition.* Women took up the campaign, centred on Birmingham and Leicester, and spread the *Immediate* message with great flair. Heyrick's late husband had been John, the brother of Ann Heyrick, who had married Aulay Macaulay, Babington's brother-in-law and Vicar of Rothley. In Babington's time three of the legal stewards of his manorial court were Heyricks. Elizabeth was treading the family path. She teamed up with Susannah Watts, who had turned to writing as a way of supplementing the very small annuity from her deceased family. For an eleven month period they published a magazine full of anti-slavery campaigning going under the charming title of *The Humming Bird.* The reason for choosing this title was to contrast the difference between the life of the slave and the bird:

> '.....deep and wide is the contrast between a gang of slaves driven to their labour by the harsh crack of the whip, or torn from their wives and children, and the little Humming Bird, buzzing like a feathered bee, free and happy to her voluntary labour, or nursing her tiny pearly eggs in security'.[4]

Susanna even wrote a poetic song on this theme, which was set to music by the wife of Babington's former manorial steward, Mrs William Heyrick, and published in *The Humming Bird.* Susannah made several visits to Rothley Temple, and preserved relics in her scrapbook, including a copy of a hymn written by Babington in 1833.

As the tide turned into the 1830s, it began to come in with a greater force than in the previous decade. The whirlwind broke in Jamaica. Twenty thousand slaves rose in revolt led by Baptist deacon Samuel Sharpe, the human and material cost was immense. More than that, what did it auger for how the slave economy could be successfully managed in the future; more of the whip, the treadmill, the torture, the scapegoating?

Back home, England was having its own storm. Exasperation at the increasingly unworkable electoral system was spilling onto the streets. In Wilberforce's own case, before he retired in 1825, he had given up the Herculean correspondence and representative task of being the voice of over 20,000 electors in mighty Yorkshire for the tiny Borough of Bramber in Sussex. The 36 burgage-holders there [propertied people] returned two members, and since Barbara Wilberforce's cousin Lord Calthorpe controlled 20 of them, he could put in who he wished. The Reform Bills, meant to remedy this and the system's other ills, were getting beached on the shores of the House of Lords. When the people of Nottingham heard in 1831 that its castle owner the Duke of Newcastle had voted down the latest Bill, they rioted, sacking his mansion on the castle rock, leaving it in flames.

At the beginning of 1832, the Jamaica uprising was finally quelled, and when faced with the latest successful Reform Bill, King William IV (the previous Duke of Clarence) reluctantly signed it into law. Reluctantly, because the pro-slavery ex-Duke knew that the huge breath of fresh talent that would enter Parliament would see the issues more clearly, fairly and realistically. And so the new tide swept in. The Anti-Slavery Committee provided evidence, lobbying, and the channel for mass support; the reformed House of Commons, with many members having first-hand experience of the brutal cost of keeping the island economies going, knew what was at stake; the slaves themselves, a veritable powder keg, waited on the mother of parliaments to give them their freedom. In the summer of 1833 the Emancipation Bill became an Act, albeit with a conditional freedom as 'apprentices' in 1834, and full freedom in 1838. But to our undying shame, Parliament had to commit £20 millions in bonds to buy out the planter's right to the property they held in their slaves. Hochschild puts this as equal to about 40% of the national budget then, an amount in today's money of £1.2 billion. Much of the money finished up in the hands of financial creditors in London who held mortgages on the plantations. Nevertheless, the 'sacredness of private property had been upheld'.[5] The Church of England's payment for the 415 slaves on its Codrington estate was £8,823. 8s. 9d., almost £500,000 today.

Late on Friday 26th July 1833 the severely ailing Wilberforce heard that the Bill had passed its Third Reading in the Commons. 'Thank God', he said 'that I have lived to witness a day in which England is willing to give twenty millions sterling for the Abolition of Slavery'.[6] He slipped away three days later, and by universal acclaim, was laid to rest in Westminster Abbey. On 5th August 1833, William Evans, an MP from Derbyshire, wrote from the Commons to Thomas Babington at Rothley Temple:[7]

> 'My Dear Friend
> I have to thank you for your two letters. As one of the oldest and most intimate friends of Mr Wilberforce, you may well have felt much on his death. We can never expect to see the like of him again. I saw him on the Saturday before his death looking so much better than I expected and with all his interests about his friends undiminished, talking with animations, rejoicing at the approaching freedom of the slaves, and highly gratified that the apprenticeship had been shortened. He could not then walk, but no immediate danger was apprehended, and little thought of following him so soon to the grave. The funeral was very solemn and imposing, even on the streets as well as in the Abbey, everybody looked as though they had lost a friend. May I and many others strive more to follow him as he followed Christ.

> I had hoped that we should have been able to shorten the apprenticeship to about three years, but we have gained much and must try to be content. God grant that all parties here and in the Colonies may act mercifully and wisely on this great occasion, and that the Freedom of the Slaves may be blessed with increasing civilisation and above all increasing True Religion.
>
> With kind regards to Mrs Babington and your Daughter
> I am, my dear friend
> very affectionately yours
> William Evans'

Four years later, on 21st November 1837, Thomas Babington died at home at Rothley among his family, aged 79. William Acworth, the Vicar he installed in Rothley Church in 1833, preached at a special service in Rothley Church on 3rd December 1837 in Babington's honour. Among his many words, he said this:[8]

> 'So truly was he clothed with humility, that I scarcely ever remember to have heard him refer to anything which he had ever done to promote the cause of religion, or the welfare of mankind. It is however probably well known that he toiled incessantly as a senator and as a private individual to promote the Abolition of Slavery, in connection with his most intimate friend Mr Wilberforce, who lived just long enough the hear its death blow struck by the British Parliament'.

'In connection with his most intimate friend, Mr Wilberforce'. Perhaps that was Babington's real contribution, that by his presence alongside the little man from Hull, to be the constant reassurance to Wilberforce that his cause was right, that justice and humanity must be allowed to win through.

Thomas Babington was buried in the Chapel at the Temple, and his wife Jean lies buried beside him.

Chapter Notes:

1 Barnes, Thomas, *Parliamentary Portraits.* P.72.
2 Matthew Babington to Thomas B., 9 Jun 1824, Babington MSS, 12.90. The dividend was allocated £2,250 to Mansfield, £1,500 to TB, and £750 to Matthew B.
3 Hochschild, p.323.
4 Quoted in Aucott, Shirley, *Susannah Watts*, p.27, from the first issue of *The Humming Bird*, Dec 1824.
5 Hochschild, p.347.
6 R.I.& S. Wilberforce, *Life of William Wilberforce*, V, p.370.
7 Babington MSS, box 20.32.
8 Ibid, box 13.2.

*The Humming Bird*
*See page 81*

*The setting for the ceremony on 25 March 2007 where a new plaque is to be added to one of the unused faces on the monument at the Rothley Court Hotel, originally Rothley Temple, to mark the Bicentenary of the Abolition of the Slave Trade.*

# *Appendix*

What is often forgotten is the part played by slaves and former slaves who by their courage and their testimony led the resistance to what has been described as one of the greatest crimes in the history of humanity. Here is the personal testimony of four former slaves.

## DAVID SPENS

*A slave was brought from Grenada to Fife in Scotland in 1768 by Dr. David Dalrymple who called him 'black Tom' and was planning to send him back to the West Indies in September 1769. The slave was baptised as 'David Spens' that month in Wemyss Parish Church and with the help of a local farmer and Church Elder and the support of several lawyers he returned to the master to declare his freedom in these words, using his own spelling:*

'I David Spens formerly called Black Tom late slave to Dr.David Dalrymple of Lindifferen heareby intimate to you the said Dr.Dalrymple that being formerly an heathen slave to you and of consequence then at your disposal but being now instructed in the Christian Religion I have embraced the same and been publicly baptised to that faith by the Reverend Mr.Harry Spens, minister of the gospel at Wemyss and so admitted to the Church of Christ established in this Kingdom and of consequence I am now by the Christian Religion Liberate and set at freedom from my old yoke, bondage, and slavery and by the laws of this Christian land there is no slavery nor vestige of slavery allowed nevertheless you take it upon you to exercise your tyrannical power over me and would dispose of me arbitrally at your despotic will and pleasure and for that end you threaten to send me abroad out of this country to the West Indies and there dispose of me for money by which you subvert the ends and designs of the Christian institution which ransoms liberty to all its members but also you would deprive our sovereign Lord the King of a good subject.

Therefore I heareby declare that from henceforth I am to leave your family and service and protest that if you shall put in execution your wicked intention or offer to put the same in execution or in any ways abetting aiding or assisting therein or any ways be accesory there or concerned in the same less or more you shall be liable in the pains and penalties of law inflicted on persons guilty of such crimes and in all the consequences of such a wicked practice and all damages or expenses for any of my Christian Brethren who shall aid and assist and protect may be put to in prosecuting you and remedying ourselves at law and therefore take instruments'.

*David Spens sought help in Edinburgh but was arrested and held in Dysart jail. He issued writs for wrongful arrest, local churches collected money for him and the miners and the salters contributed to his costs. In the middle of the court case to determine his future Dalymple died and he was a free man.*

## OTTOBAH CUGOANA

*Quobna Ottobah Cugoano, usually known by the shorter form Ottobah Cugoano, was born in present-day Ghana in the 1750s. Kidnapped and taken into slavery, he worked on plantations in Granada before being brought to England, where he obtained his freedom. He wrote his* Thoughts and Sentiments on the Evil and Wicked Traffic of the Commerce of the Human Species, *the first directly abolitionist publication in English by an African, which was published in 1787.*

'I was born in the city of Agimaque, on the coast of Fantyn; my father was a companion to the chief in that part of the country of Fantee, and when the old king died I was left in his house with his family..... I was sent for to visit an uncle, who lived at a considerable distance from Agimaque..... we went into the woods as usual; but we had not been above two hours before our troubles began, when several great ruffians came upon us suddenly. Some of us attempted in vain to run away, but pistols and cutlasses were soon introduced, threatening, that if we offered to stir we should all lie dead on the spot. One of them pretended to be more friendly than the rest, and said, that he would speak to their lord to get us clear, and desired that we should follow him; we were then immediately divided into different parties, and drove after him. We were soon led out of the way which we knew, and towards the evening [...] we came in sight of a town, they told us that this great man of theirs lived there. Next day we travelled on, and in the evening came to a town, where I saw several white people, which made me afraid that they would eat me, according to our notion as children in the inland parts of the country. This made me rest very uneasy all the night.

After I was ordered out, the horrors I soon saw and felt, cannot be well described; I saw many of my miserable countrymen chained two and two, some hand-cuffed, and some with their hands tied behind. But when a vessel arrived to conduct us away to the ship, it was a most horrible scene; there was nothing to be heard but rattling of chains, smacking of whips, and the groans and cries of our fellow-men. Some would not stir from the ground, when they were lashed and beat in the most horrible manner. I have forgot the name of this infernal fort; but we were taken in the ship that came for us, to another that was ready to sail from Cape Coast. But it would be needless to give a description of all the horrible scenes which we saw, and the base treatment which we met with in this dreadful captive situation, as the similar cases of thousands, which suffer by this infernal traffic, are well known. Let it suffice to say, that I was thus lost to my dear indulgent parents and relations, and they to me'.

## OLAUDAH EQUIANO

*The ex-slave who also called himself 'Gustavus Vasa the African' (a reference to the great Swedish king) became one of the most celebrated advocates of the abolition of the slave trade. He toured Britain in 1792, promoting his book* The Interesting Narrative *and other writings. A convert to Methodism, Equiano listened to the debate on the slave trade in the General Assembly of the Church of Scotland that year and wrote enthusiastically to the Glasgow Courier about it. He married an Englishwoman, had two* daughters, *and died in 1797. This is part of an account in his book of life on a slave ship:*

'At last, when the ship we were in had got in all her cargo, they made ready with many fearful noises, and we were all put under deck, so that we could not see how they managed the vessel. But this disappointment was the least of my sorrow. The stench of the hold while we were on the coast was so intolerably loathsome, that it was dangerous to remain there for any time, and some of us had been permitted to stay on the deck for the fresh air; but now that the whole ship's cargo were confined together, it became absolutely pestilential. The closeness of the place, and the heat of the climate, added to the number in the ship, which was so crowded that each had scarcely room to turn himself, almost suffocated us. This produced copious perspirations, so that the air soon became unfit for respiration, from a variety of loathsome smells, and brought on a sickness among the slaves, of which many died, thus falling victims to the improvident avarice, as I may call it, of their purchasers.

This wretched situation was again aggravated by the galling of the chains, now become insupportable; and the filth of the necessary tubs, into which the children often fell, and were almost suffocated. The shrieks of the women, and the groans of the dying, rendered the whole a scene of horror almost inconceivable. Happily perhaps for myself I was soon reduced so low here that it was thought necessary to keep me almost always on deck; and from my extreme youth I was not put in fetters. In this situation I expected every hour to share the fate of my companions, some of whom were almost daily brought upon deck at the point of death, which I began to hope would soon put an end to my miseries. Often did I think many of the inhabitants of the deep much more happy than myself, I envied them the freedom they enjoyed, and as often wished I could change my condition for theirs. Every circumstance I met with served only to render my state more painful, and heighten my apprehensions, and my opinion of the cruelty of the whites'.

## IGNATIUS SANCHO

*Ignatius Sancho is thought to have been born a slave on a ship crossing the Atlantic from Africa to the West Indies. His earliest memories were of Greenwich, near London, where he worked as a child slave. Later he worked as a butler, ran a grocery shop, composed music, and appeared on the stage. The first African we know of to vote in a British election, he wrote a large number of letters which were published after his death. Here is an extract from one of them to his friend Jack Wingate, London bookseller in 1778.*

'I am sorry to observe that the practice of your country (which as a resident I love - and for its freedom - and for the many blessings I enjoy in it - shall ever have my warmest wishes - prayers - and blessings); I say it is with reluctance, that I must observe your country's conduct has been uniformly wicked in the East - West Indies - and even on the coast of Guinea. - The grand object of English navigators - indeed of all christian navigators - is money - money - money - for which I do not pretend to blame them - Commerce was meant by the goodness of the Deity to diffuse the various goods of the earth into every part - to unite mankind in the blessed chains of brotherly love - society - and mutual dependence: - the enlightened Christian should diffuse the riches of the Gospel of peace - with the commodities of his respective land - Commerce attended with strict honesty - and with Religion for its companion - would be a blessing to every shore it touched at.

In Africa, the poor wretched natives - blessed with the most fertile and luxuriant soil - are rendered so much the more miserable for what Providence meant as a blessing: - the Christians' abominable traffic for slaves - and the horrid cruelty and treachery of the petty Kings - encouraged by their Christian customers - who carry them strong liquors - to enflame their national madness - and powder - and bad fire-arms - to furnish them with the hellish means of killing and kidnapping. - But enough - it is a subject that sours my blood - and I am sure will not please the friendly bent of your social affections. - I mentioned these only to guard my friend against being too hasty in condemning the knavery of a people who bad as they may be -

possibly - were made worse by their Christian visitors. - Make human nature thy study - wherever thou residest - whatever the religion - or the complexion - study their hearts. - Simplicity, kindness, and charity be thy guard - with these even savages will respect you - and God will bless you'.

## *Abolition of the British Slave Trade: A Timeline in Parliament*

| | |
|---|---|
| 1776-1778/9 | Wilberforce, Babington, and Thomas Gisborne at Cambridge together |
| 1780 | Wilberforce at age 21 becomes MP for Hull |
| 1781 | William Pitt the Younger becomes MP at age 22 |
| Mid-May 1787 | Wilberforce agrees to the the urgings of Pitt and Grenville to lead the cause in the Commons |
| Late May 1787 | London Abolition Committee formed (9 Quakers, 3 Anglicans)<br>Thomas Clarkson goes on the road gathering evidence and witnesses |
| Spring 1788 | Pitt as Prime Minister quietly commissions the Privy Council to investigate the Trade |
| Autumn 1788 | Dolben's Act regulates the number of slaves that can be squeezed onto slave ships |
| Spring 1789 | Pitt and the Speaker Grenville work out twelve resolutions that could build into a bill. Wilberforce launches the debate with a three and a half hour speech. The resolutions never get properly put, the House in the end deciding to send the matter to its own Committee to gather evidence, as it was *demeaning to itself* to rely on Privy Council evidence [from the Lords] |
| July 1789 | The Bastille is stormed in Paris. Revolution begins |

| | |
|---|---|
| Jan 1790 | Wilberforce by a subtle manoeuvre has the unworkable whole-house Committee translated into an efficient Select Committee. By June, hundreds of pages of evidence are accumulated |
| Jun 1790 | General Election |
| Summer 1790 | Wilberforce, Babington and Gisborne at Yoxall worked weeks of nine-hour days checking, abridging, and building a case from *14 hundred folios* of the Select Committee Evidence |
| Spring 1791 | More evidence gathered. London Committee helps with the analysis |
| April 1791 | Babington & Gisborne at Wilberforce's home, Old Palace Yard, Westminster, helping with speech preparation |
| 19/20 Apr 1791 | Abolition Bill lost 163-88 |
| Summer 1791 | Wilberforce at Rothley with Babington thinking it all through again |
| Spring 1792 | Babington and Gisborne at Wilberforce's London home as his 'staffers' |
| April 1792 | Abolition Bill passed 230-85, but with an amendment from immediate to *Gradual* abolition. The bill moves into a fog of indecision about *when*, with the House of Lords setting out on its own long trail of hearing evidence |

| | |
|---|---|
| 1793-1802 | The French revolutionary war. Pitt and Parliament becomes much pre-occupied with fighting the war, particularly in its overseas offshoots |
| 1800 | Babington becomes Member of Parliament for Leicester. Wilberforce's unofficial PPS in the Commons |
| 1805 | French and Spanish fleets defeated at Trafalgar |
| 1806 | James Stephen suggests a clever Bill to Wilberforce which passes quickly and unnoticed. It allowed the British navy to seize the cargoes of neutral-flagged ships which were supporting the trading of Britain's enemies. Cuts the Slave Trade in half because many neutral ships were in reality British |
| 1806 | Pitt dies. General Election |
| Spring 1807 | Lord Grenville now Prime Minister, who with speaker Howick, agrees to launch Abolition Bill in the Lords first. In February it passes the Commons 283-16. Signed into law on 25 March 1807 |
| 1815 | End of Napoleonic wars |
| 1817 | Slave Registration Bill. Slaves listed every two years |
| 1818 | Babington at 60 retires from Parliament |
| 1823 | Anti-Slavery Society formed in London and begins active campaigning for *Gradual* Emancipation |

| | |
|---|---|
| 1824 | Elizabeth Heyrick in Leicester publishes the pamphlet *Immediate not Gradual Abolition* |
| 1825 | Wilberforce at 66 retires from Parliament. Thomas Fowell Buxton continues to lead the Parliamentary campaign for Emancipation |
| 1831 | Major slave revolt in Jamaica, brutally suppressed. |
| 1832 | Reform Bill passes. Parliament is reconstituted from a more representative electorate |
| Summer 1833 | Abolition of Slavery Bill passed. Wilberforce dies on 29 July, three days later |
| 1 Aug 1834 | Emancipation Day. Provides that most slaves then serve a further four year *apprenticeship* |

# *Bibliography & Sources*

*Extensive and regular reference has been made to the well known books on this topic. Where actual text is quoted, single inverted commas are used. From time to time the interesting primary sources cited in the reference texts are used unattributed. Manuscript sources specially consulted for the publication are cited in full. The material in the Macaulay chapters are drawn from Iain Whyte's own book, 'Scotland and the Abolition of Black Slavery, 1756-1838', from extensive study of such manuscript sources as those at the Huntingdon Library, California and the British Library, and from private papers in the hands of the Macaulay family.*

Reference Texts:

Charles Booth, *Zachary Macaulay, His part in the movement for the Abolition of the Slave Trade and of Slavery,* (London, 1934).
Holland, M., (Viscountess Knutsford), *The Life and Letters of Zachary Macaulay*, (London, 1900).
Hochschild, Adam, *Bury the Chains*, Pan Books, (London 2005).
Oldfield, J.R., *Popular Politics and British Anti-Slavery: The Mobilisation of Public Opinion against the Slave Trade 1787-1807*, (Manchester, 1995).
Pollock, John, *William Wilberforce,* Lion Publishing, (London 1986).
Walvin, J., *England, Slaves and Freedom 1776-1838*, (Jackson, MS, 1986).

Manuscript Sources and other Texts:

Aucott, Shirley, *Susannah Watts 1768-1842*, (Leicester 2004).
Babington MSS, Trinity College, Cambridge.(51 Boxes).
Booth, Charles, *Zachary Macaulay: His part in the Movement for the Abolition of the Slave Trade and of Slavery* (London, 1934).
*Clapham & the Clapham Sect*, Clapham Antiquarian Society, (1927).
Thomas Clarkson, *A History of the Rise, Progress, and Accomplishment of the Abolition of the African Slave Trade by the British Parliament.* vol. 1, pp.208-209, 214-215.

Fielding, Sir John, *Extracts from such of the Penal Laws as Particularly Relate to the Peace & Good Order of this Metropolis* (London, 1768, pp143-145..

Macaulay, Zachary, *Negro Slavery or A View of Some of the more Prominent Features of that State of Society as it exists in the United States of America and in the Colonies of the West Indies especially in Jamaica* (London,1823).

Macaulay Papers (22 Boxes) The Huntington Library, San Marino, California.

Oxford Dictionary of National Biography, (2004).

Shylon, Folarin O, *Black Slaves in Britain*, London: Institute of Race Relations/Oxford University Press (1874).

Trevelyan, G.O., *The Life and Letters of Lord Macaulay*, Harper, (New York, 1876).

Trevelyan, G. M., *English Social History*, Longmans 1945.

Wilberforce, R. I. & S., ed., *Correspondence of William Wilberforce*, 5 volumes, 1838.

Williams, *Capitalism and Slavery*, (London, 1944).